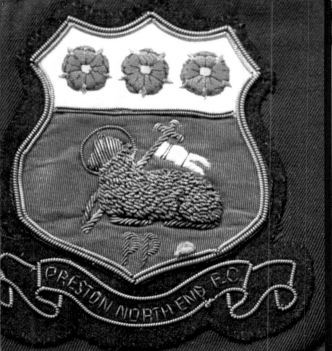

CW01082030

P.N.E.

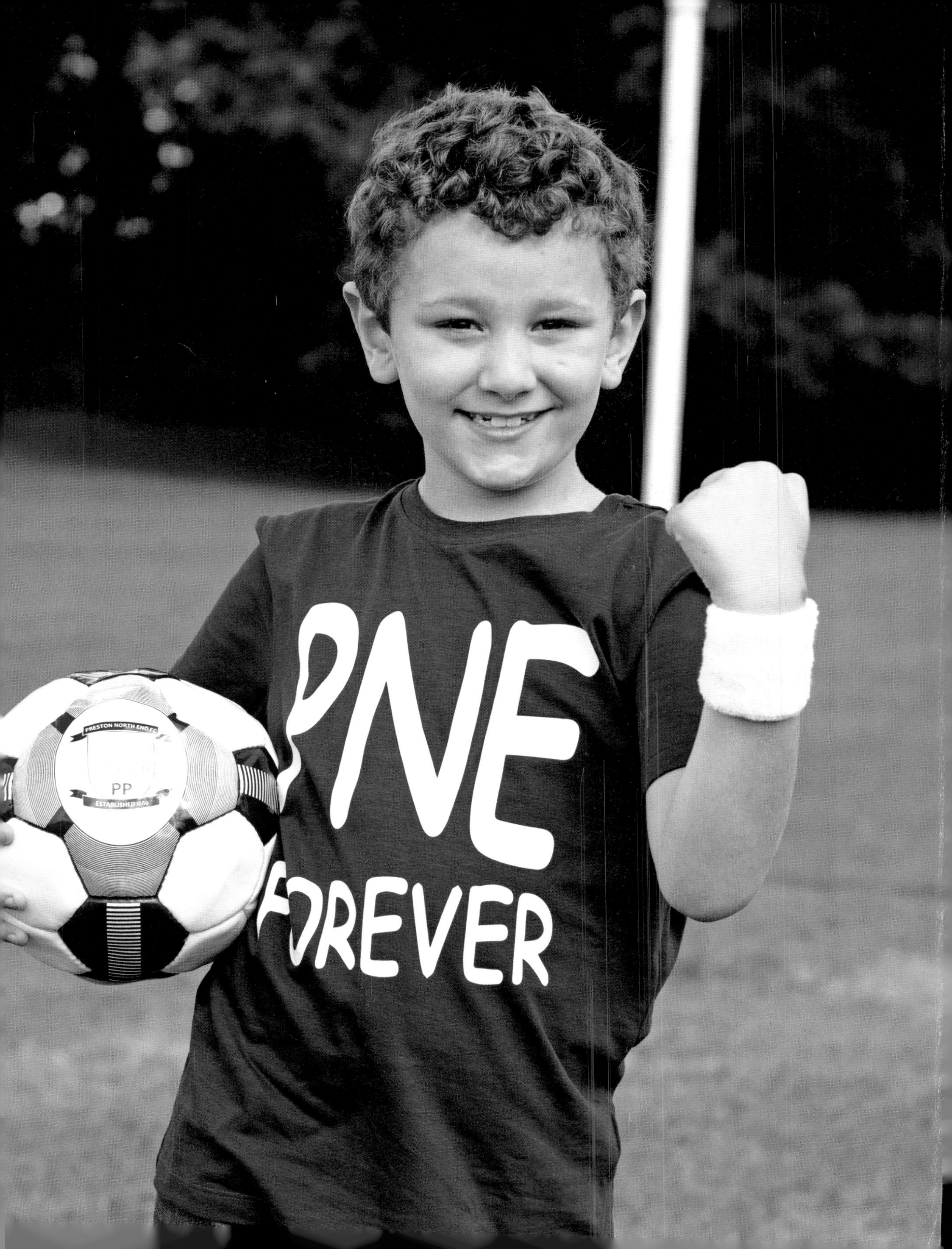
PNE
FOREVER
PRESTON NORTH END FC
PP
ESTABLISHED 1880

P N E

STORIES FROM THE FANS OF
PRESTON
NORTH
END

F O R -

Presented by
Michael Barrett

E V E R

BEN CASEY

I grew up in the terraced streets in Deepdale and some of my earliest memories are of dark winter nights when thousands of people would descend on our area. They would always be in high spirits as they headed for a large, strange looking building that would light up and groan and roar. As soon as I was old enough, I started going to matches with my friends, usually dependent on if we'd managed to collect enough for 'looking after' people's cars. The first season I started going regularly when I was still only eight. We (regular fans are allowed to say 'we') finished runners-up in the First Division (now the Premiership). We then started on a long, drawn out but steady decline until 1986 when we finished next to bottom of the Fourth Division and had to apply for re-election.

Only real football fans would understand why I never for one minute considered jumping ship and following another club, despite my work causing me to live a couple of miles from Old Trafford for four years and only a stone's throw from Highbury in the season when Arsenal won the double. And only real football fans who have had a Catholic upbringing would understand why it seemed obvious to me that this dramatic decline was all my fault. My indiscretions had caused the famous Preston North End, first champions of the oldest league in the world, to be languishing at the bottom of the Fourth Division.

I needed to put things right.

So, I started to design a new stadium with all sorts of new ideas that I thought would help point North End back in the right direction. Not being an architect didn't deter me. I gave myself a crash course in modern stadia design and pinched the structural engineering from the stadium in Genoa, Italy.

In a classic case of naivety being the driving force behind progress, I had a massive breakthrough. I came across Bryan Gray, one of the few people who could take these ideas and turn them into reality. I presented to him, he took on the project and told me to get on with it. Working with a small team, in which I would have to single out David Robinson, it all came together remarkably quickly.

I hope that all the supporters whose fantastic stories are featured in this book are proud of their stadium and they're happy I've now served my 'penance'.

I hope that one day in the not too distant future, we'll see Premier League football played there. My own greatest memory of Deepdale will always be having seen Sir Tom Finney play. I was very young and he was in the twilight of his career but I can distinctly remember the crowd going eerily silent each time he received the ball in the expectation that something remarkable was about to happen, and invariably, it did.

What a great club we are.

Ben Casey

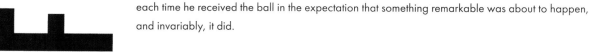

MICHAEL BARRETT

What makes a club? Its players, its stadium, its history?

Its fans?

From the early days of Victorian football, when men and women stood on wooden planks on raised earth, all the way through to today's deluxe all-seater stadiums, football has been synonymous with its fans. In those halcyon days, when North End ruled the world, football grew to become the sport of the masses, a winter release for the oppressed working class. In 1850 The Factory Act decreed a Saturday 2pm finish in factories and mills, and thus a 3pm kick-off allowed ample time for keen football folk to return home and get ready for the match. And get ready they did. The love affair took root and, whilst fashions and fan culture may have changed, the way we react to 'Association Football' has undoubtedly not.

Now I must stress, whether you'd been on one match or one hundred, it didn't matter for this book. This is in no way a compilation of who I consider to be North End's greatest fans. I don't believe in such things. Instead, please view this as a simple snapshot of our fan base (by a pretend photographer). Initially I planned to interview seventy North Enders but, as my network grew, so too did the recommendations, and seventy quickly became ninety, then one hundred, until eventually I had to stop as the book was getting too big and I was running out of time!

So what does football mean to us fans today, and vice-versa? Ever since the days of the great William Sudell, football has been a business, but it's a financial transaction like no other. We pay our money, lend our support and in return are gifted a range of emotions – some emotions more than others. Nothing has changed. If it takes a hold, it can stay with you forever and you become the bearer of an invisible flame, standing side by side with generations through time. During my interviews, three words kept cropping up: passion, community, family. Each Saturday when interviewing fans, I'd witness many cheery interactions and quiet acts of kindness amongst the North End faithful. No fanfare, no fuss, just people looking out for each other. In other words, a real community. Then COVID struck, the games stopped, and the world changed. Never before has the bond between clubs and their fans been so highlighted. And when the time came, Preston North End were not found wanting. Those words: passion, community, family, were never more apt as our players, management and fans united to show just why we are called 'Proud Preston'.

To present these interviews is my honour. It's been an absolute pleasure to have spent time with these fans and listen to their stories, and I'm extremely grateful to everyone who has given their time to be interviewed. I've enjoyed every one of them, and I hope you do too.

We are the one and only North End. These are our stories.

Michael Barrett

CONTENTS

SENIOR

1

WHITES

DAVID COULTON

My Grandmother, Grace Sibbert, helped to start The Dick, Kerr Ladies. In October 1917 the factory lads team challenged the ladies to a match and Grace quickly accepted, helped to form a team and played in their first ever game.

I started going on North End in 1957-58 when I was eight. I used to go with my Aunty who was Grace Sibbert's adopted daughter.

My Aunty was only about 4ft 9 inches and went through the juveniles' turnstile even though she was in her thirties. She would cling on behind me and they thought she was a young girl. She'd then go up towards the top of the old Kop next to the wall, and a load of old fellas and I'd go down to the Lowthorpe Road corner. I had a little camping seat, my bobble hat and a rattle and I'd climb over the railings onto the cinder track.

They let the kids sit right up close to the touchline but you weren't allowed on the grass. As long as there was enough room for the policeman to walk past you were alright. People walked around with big trays selling treacle toffee. Fans would pass their two bob down through the crowd and the seller would then pass a bag of treacle up. Probably most of it had gone by the time it reached the buyer!

In the 50s and 60s lots of fans used to come on bicycles and the houses behind the Kop had signs up, 'Park your bicycle here' and, 'Threepence for a bike'. It was crammed. All these driveways would be full of cycles piled on top of one another. After the match, everyone was rushing out of the gates for their bikes. Cycles were being tossed up in the air.

'That's mine!', 'Yep, that one's mine!'

It was chaos, but nothing was ever stolen.

In 1961-62 we drew Liverpool in round five of the FA Cup. After two draws, it went to a third match to be played at Old Trafford. I didn't know we were going, but the morning of the game my Aunty left a note saying, 'When you've finished school we're going to the match on the Bon Chaunce coach.'

That night there was a snow storm all the way to Manchester and a blizzard throughout the game in which Peter Thomson scored a brilliant winner.

Afterwards, with the weather, we couldn't find the coach park and by the time we did, the coach had left! We had our North End hats and scarves on and decided to walk back towards Manchester to see if we could get home to Preston, so we're walking through the dock road and we turn round and see the North End coach going along slowly due to the weather.

Stood at the back of the coach are some gentlemen who turned out to be Liverpool and PNE directors discussing Peter Thompson signing for Liverpool. He signed that night and joined 'em the following season. Next thing, another coach came down and stopped with us in its headlights.

The door opened and down the steps came Charlie Lea who was of West Indian origin, one of the first Black players at PNE. Although he never made the first team, I knew him well from the reserves. Charlie was always smiling. Anyway, he gets down off the bus and says, 'What you doing, you two?' So we told him and he said, 'oh, get on't bus, you two!' So me and my Aunty travelled back with the reserves that night and I told all the kids at school the next day!

DAVID HILL

When I was an apprentice, Tom Finney would come into the shop where I worked. I used to put the cape on him, comb his hair through and say, 'The boss will be along in a minute.' and he would always say, 'Thank you, son.'

Then years later, when I'd been in business for quite a long time myself, he walked in one quiet afternoon, sat down and had a haircut. If somebody had come in I would've asked Sir Tom if I could have a photo with him but nobody came in! That was the only time I cut his hair and nobody saw it, but I know.

Where I used to work, they had pictures of Tom Finney in the window. Joe Walton was another and Charlie Wayman. They all had a quiff. You'd get lads coming in with football programmes asking for the same styles as the players. Sir Tom had his hair with a nice wave. 'I want it like Tommy Finney with a wave.' Or sometimes they'd bring in record albums. 'Can I have it like Perry Como?' That's how we barbers learned our trade.

After the game on a Saturday, fans would come rushing in to get their hair done for that night and it would be, 'The referee this, the referee that, bleep, bleep, bleep!' And one day I said to my boss, 'Is it always the referee?' He said, 'No, Preston are just a rotten team!'

'Alan Kelly Senior had a go at hairdressing and so did Alex Dawson.'

This was during their football careers and they worked for Vin Miller who was a great hairdresser. It was brilliant publicity. Howard Kendall tried it too.

I remember a North West comp in Blackpool. I was in the Intermediates and Alan Kelly was in the Apprentices.

The judges come round to judge appearance and style and check if it's straight and level and when they got to Alan Kelly's model, one was asked, 'What do you think of that, Tommy?' and he replied, 'Marvellous goalkeeper' and walked off.

Before I opened this shop in 1981, I had another in a different part of Deepdale in the late 60s and 70s. PNE players, John Smith, Ricky Thomson, Eric Snookes, John Bird, the Baxter Brothers, they were all clients of mine and came in together after training.

One day Stuart Baxter said, 'I'm getting married the day after the last day of the season, will you do my hair that morning?' I said, 'Of course.' He then said, 'there'll be me and my brother, Mick, my dad and my younger brother. They'll all want doing.'

Well, I'd already arranged to go for a Sunday lunch that day with my Wife and Grandma at 12:30. Anyway, the Baxters got in at 10am and then more arrived asking, 'Can you do mine?', 'Can you do mine too?' They all had a lot of hair in those days and it was a lot of cutting and styling, plus I was on my own. Ploughing through all these long mullets trying to get them dry as quickly as possible, it was hilarious!

This PNE tea towel I have in the shop, I took it to the top of Kilimanjaro when I was fifty. I've done a lot of mountains: The Yosemite, the Atlas. My Granddaughter got meningitis and when she got better, I felt we owed the research people a lot for helping her so I did Kilimanjaro for the meningitis charity. If I'd had that PNE gnome back then, I would have taken that up too!

DAVID HODKINSON

My Dad always came on Preston North End with his dad. They were both keen supporters of North End and England. I remember we had a massive red rosette in the house that my Dad used to wear when he was going down to Wembley to watch England play back in the day.

Sadly, my Dad went down with his ship in March 1943 when I was only seven months old and so it was my Grandad who first brought me on North End when I was just four. My Grandad took me on along with many other people from Aberdeen Street where we lived. It was slap bang off Deepdale Road and Peel Hall Street, and many of the people on the Town End came from round that area.

As kids, we used to sit on the railings at the match and I remember having a rattle which made a heck of a racket!

'We also used to play footy on the area outside the old West Stand. That was our pitch.'

We'd use the West Stand gates as goals but those gates were so big, if you were in goal you had no chance of saving anything!

Tommy Docherty was one of my favourites back then. He lived on Lincoln Street near us and would always be very generous when we put our Guy Fawkes out on Peel Hall Street. Bobbie Beattie was another favourite along with Willie Cunningham and of course Sir Tom.

One year, when the club were really stuck for money, a group of fans, including myself and John Tracey, helped out by painting the ground. John was a very good friend of mine and was a fantastic supporter of PNE, going to every single game and every single football ground in England. Sadly, John passed away at a young age, but he is fondly remembered by many fans. I have happy memories of us

painting the stanchions that day and for our reward we got a pie! But we did get a lot of thanks as well from the staff.

I'm very passionate about North End and that's mainly because of how I was brought up. In the 80-81 season I went to our final game away at Derby's old ground. We won but got relegated because Cardiff managed a 0-0 draw against West Ham. At the time, we ran a hotel in Blackpool and when I got back that night everybody was joking and one of our guests had actually made a coffin and placed it in the bar area with flowers around it. Looking back, I can see it was quite funny, but I really didn't see the funny side at the time!

I was always a big Town End supporter but we changed because we were fortunate to have made good friends with a PNE player who one day very kindly gave us season tickets for the Pavilion. The good thing was that, from that day onwards, my Wife, Anne, came on with me and we've been going on every game together ever since. Anne is Prestonian born and bred and it was fantastic when she decided to come and watch PNE with me.

We sit in the STF stand these days and we're very proud to say that we selected our seats from a drawing before the stand was built. We actually used to see Sir Tom quite often with his good lady and we'd have a chat about the games. He was just an all-round fantastic man as well as one of the world's best ever players. His statue is perhaps the finest in football and is a fitting tribute. He will never be forgotten by Preston fans, I'm sure of that.

Photo: David & Anne Hodkinson

DOROTHY ALICE DAWSON

Football was always around when I were growing up. My Dad, Albert Leeming, was a footballer and played for Darwen FC. In 1932 they reached the FA Cup third round and were drawn to play Arsenal on the 9th January.

It was lucky he ever went as Mum was pregnant with me and I was due on that day but I was born on the 8th and they sent a telegram down to him in London to say I had arrived. The players were staying at The Strand Hotel and going to see all the top shows. My name, Dorothy Alice, well, the initials – D. A. – they stand for Darwen and Arsenal, my Dad's idea!

'My first ever match at Preston North End I went on the Spion Kop. I can see it now. Oh, it was magical!'

I lived on Havelock Street near the Moor Park gates and we'd walk to the game along Moor Park Avenue. There used to be big crowds of people walking that avenue on match days.

At Deepdale, I had a regular spot on the Kop on one of the corners where they put the half-time scores up. I used to perch myself on top of the railings. It was a handy spot. Then one day I was so intrigued in the game when suddenly . . . BANG! The ball hit me flat in the face and knocked me flying off the railings. I never sat there again after that. I was so embarrassed.

The best player I ever saw was Tom Finney. He was magic. They used to say, 'Give it to Tom, he'll score!' Bill Shankly was great too. I remember chasing him for his autograph.

He lived on Deepdale Road by the County Arms. I got it too! I used to chase them all for autographs. I was football mad.

When I was fifteen I actually played a match for the Dick, Kerr Ladies. My Grandfather was a friend of Pop Frankland who looked after the team, and it was him that got me to go and play for them. This particular match was a charity match away at Hyde on a Monday morning. They told me the coach would pick me up at the Moor Park gates between 8:30-9:00am.

On the morning when I was waiting, I suddenly realised, my god, they're all going to school. Park School on Moor Park Avenue, it was my school. All the children were going to school and I was taking the day off to play football! But I didn't think they'd miss me for one day. Anyway, I played and we had a really good time. But when I got back my Mum said I've not to go to school until she's been in to see the Head Mistress. I asked why.

'Because your English teacher saw you going on the coach to play football and reported you!'

When I went back, the Head Mistress – she was a tough one – said, 'I don't like having to do this to one of my girls but I'm going to have to suspend you or let you go altogether! You have two options, either pack up football – it's not ladylike – or continue your studies and stay on at school.' I had no choice. I couldn't finish school at fifteen, so that was it.

I played outside-left that day – Sir Tom's position.

GEORGE GREEN

At school, the teacher would get complimentary tickets for the North End and if you'd been a good lad you had a chance of getting one. It were only way we could go as we had no money to spend.

My first game was around 1937. I'd be about ten, and a few of us lads from school got tickets. It was Moor Park Methodist. We'd always be out playin' football on't cobbles at playtime.

My Dad played for Southport and Halifax but before them was at PNE. He played a lot for the reserves but just once for the first team. It was in 1921 and he actually made a goal. Oh aye, crossed it for Jefferis to nod in! He used to say that at home, 'I put it over and he just had to nod it in.' Ha!

Tommy Roberts was his favourite. He was a brilliant goal scorer and he had a pub too, The Stephenson's Arms. We lived just a block away from there. I think that's why he was his favourite. Dad is on a PNE team photo next to Tommy Roberts. I had it but lost it then it appeared in the paper. Gave me the surprise of my life.

When I grew up, I also played a lot so I couldn't go on Deepdale on Saturdays. But if there were any cup ties mid-week, we were always there and we'd go on the reserves too. They got big crowds for reserve matches back then.

'I was a centre-forward and inside-forward. I played for PNE A & B Teams and also for Bentham, and Chorley.'

I stopped playing in my thirties so then I could follow North End full time. In the 1950s, I was living on Hammond Street and used to walk to the ground

up Moor Park Avenue. On match days there'd be thousands walking up there. There were no motor cars then and people were selling things. Blokes with trays selling toys and mementoes of North End. It was about 9p to get in and I mostly stood on the Spion Kop.

I had a blue and white scarf, but I wasn't one of these with a fancy hat or 'owt like that. It was surprising, every time you went on, the same crowd of people were around you including quite a few young ladies and if anybody started swearing then t'other lads would get on to 'em and shout, 'Eh! Less o' that!'

The players that stand out from then? Tommy Finney of course. He was the greatest. Jimmy Dougal, Angus Morrison, little Harry Anders, he was a good player, and usually Tom's replacement. When they announced, 'At no.7: Harry Anders', there'd be a massive groan around the ground because it meant Tom wasn't playing. It were terrible really, and Harry was a real wholehearted player. He'd put himself about. They'd delay announcing the team until they were sure everyone was in the ground before saying Tom wasn't playing!

I saw Shanks. He was a good hard man, a grafter, a real team player. He'd go in hard! Tommy Smith was a great centre-half. Jimmy Milne was good. Ha! I've seen 'em all. And Georgie Mutch, who scored that extra-time winner in 1938. I remember 'em doing the tour in an open top bus with the Cup at the front. We were at New Hall Lane, because my Uncle lived up there, and all the people had lined the streets. That was the last time the FA Cup was in Preston. Oh, happy days . . . Happy days they were for sure!

HARRY BILLINGTON

I remember one character, we called him the 'Razor Blade King'. He was a smart dressed fella with a brown felt bowler hat, not a black one, and he had this bag, and they reckon if somebody shouted for razor blades he could toss 'em up into the crowd for somebody to catch.

He started selling pens too, and went to every ground round here when North End were away. At the back of the Town End there were programme sellers and a caravan selling pies. At half-time, if you got a programme you could make out the scores through the letters board. They had a board at the Pavilion where the players came out and another directly opposite at the West Stand but you had to have a programme to know the games and the letters.

I went on the Town End. I've always gone on the Town End. There used to be these concrete pillars with two bars and, well, all the kids sat on there. Then when it were full they'd let 'em sit on the gravel.

I always went early. I'd be on for one o'clock to get this particular spot which were nearly right at centre of goals and I'd have my rattle and a scarf

'In them days, your Grandmother or someone would knit you a scarf, and everybody had these rattles which were really redundant stock from the war.'

They were from the ARP Wardens who would go round the streets spinning the rattles telling people to get inside or into the air raid shelters so they must have had thousands in stock. Now they'd be a lethal weapon.

Oh, they were a noise; my Dad used to say, 'Stop that in house!' At the cup final there were 100,000 fans, so imagine all the rattles. Oh, the noise! Aye, good days.

I remember me Dad's Uncle, my Great Uncle George. In them days our family, all my aunts and uncles, all lived on the same street on Chester Road. George had been in the First World War and he'd been gassed, you know, and as he got older it affected him. He became bedfast and they put his bed downstairs and my Grandmother used to go across to look after him. A fella from round the corner called Bill Salisbury also used to visit him and they'd talk about football before the war.

When North End were playing at Rovers, they used to walk it and go in half the pubs along the way. They'd talk about Dickie Bond, Tommy Roberts and all these players. I can remember to this day, I was sat near the fire and they were talking and puffing on a pipe, and I'll never forget it. Bill said, 'Do you know George, we've seen 'em all ant we? But by the bloomin' 'ell, that Tom Finney is better than the bloody lot of em. Better than Alex James."

Well, Alex James was the kingpin, but they reckon when he first came on everybody laughed because of his long baggy shorts, but they say he were brilliant when he got the ball. I think my Great Uncle and Bill had also seen some of the old Invincibles: Geordie Drummond, Bob Holmes and all of them. It was good listening to them, they knew all the names. I vaguely remember seeing Bob Holmes myself. He lived on Deepdale Road right near the ground and I think he did a bit of gardening for North End. I remember seeing him because somebody ran over for his autograph and he wouldn't give it. He said sorry, but his days of playing football were finished. Aye, Bob Holmes, a Preston bloke, and a great full-back I believe.

JOHN WILSON

One of my earliest memories goes back to 1958 when my friend, Billy and I would play football in the street with a tennis ball, kicking it against the gable wall.

One Saturday, Billy's Dad gave us two shillings and said North End were playing Newcastle. At the time it was only a shilling each for juniors which is about 5p now. We lost 4-3 and I can remember coming off and saying we should've won and Billy saying Newcastle were better. We were arguing like mad!

What sticks in my mind was that Newcastle had a distinctive white trim around their shorts and a black and white trim around the top of their sock, much like the old band around a policeman's hat. Anyway, after that I was converted and would go on whenever I had any spending money. I didn't rely on Billy's Dad to give me a shilling. I got a paper round so I could pay to go on.

I saw Sir Tom play in my younger days when I probably didn't appreciate just how good he was technically, but I have to say, my favourite player was Peter Thompson. He was so skilful and so quick. In the warm-ups he used to do juggling and tricks. He could do all kinds of stuff with the ball.

In February '62 we played Liverpool in the FA Cup and it went to a second replay which was a night match at Old Trafford. I hadn't told my parents I was going and I only had two and six in money, so I jumped the train to Manchester. Shankly was Liverpool's manager and they had Ian St John, Ron Yeats and Roger Hunt, but it was our Peter Thompson who scored the winner.

About two-thirds into the second half, he picked up the ball in the inside-left position and hit a screamer right in the top corner. I jumped up, jubilant, and started cheering then I noticed everyone around me was silent. I hadn't realised I was in the Liverpool end! When the game restarted I slowly drifted away from that area.

Back home, as I walked up the ramp at Preston Station, the ticket officer asked, 'Where's your ticket, son?' I said, 'Oh, my Dad's got it, he's just behind me . . .' and I got through. Sorry, British Rail.

I can remember Franny Burns who played on the left side of midfield. He got so much stick from supporters that I would spend most of the match defending him. He was a really good player. I couldn't count the number of goals he made for Mike Elwiss and Alex Bruce. He used to drive balls through crisply at knee height and Brucey would just need to swivel and bang them in on the volley. It was great to see.

About ten years ago, I was invited to the famous allotment shed after a comment I'd put in The Evening Post. Unfortunately, Sir Tom couldn't make it that day but Tommy Thompson was there and Les Dagger and Leo Gornall.

They had a kitchen alongside the huts and Leo and Les were making bacon butties and cups of tea. Inside, the shed walls were pasted with newspaper headlines and posters of PNE. We just sat there eating butties, drinking tea and talking football. It was fantastic!

'For me, PNE are a passion and it grieves me when I see kids in other clubs' shirts in the town centre.'

I can't understand it. Preston is my town and PNE are my team. It means a lot. There's no other. They're my home team. It runs deep.

JOYCE & OLIVE WATSON

Dad had a fish and chip shop and he used to drive us to Deepdale. Mum would go to Grandad's in Ashton and then we'd meet her at the end of New Hall Lane when we were coming home.

In those days not many women really went to football, let alone play it. It was a couple of years before Tom Finney finished. Dad went in the old West Stand and we'd go in the Paddock. The Brindle Brass band used to sit in front of the Paddock on a long bench. We were so small we could barely see over the railings and the band members used to lift us over and sit us with them on the bench. If there wasn't enough room, we'd sit on their knees! They used to play 'Margie' when the team came out. That was the main one, and they'd march up and down the pitch.

We were about fourteen when we started going regularly and had scarves which we knitted ourselves and embroidered all the players' names on. We knitted gloves and hats too. We didn't have money to get those things back then and they weren't readily available to buy either. If you wanted a scarf the only place selling them was Willie Cunningham's sports shop on Church Street.

Oh, and we had a rattle! I remember us taking that rattle to Villa Park when we played Swansea in the semi-final in 1964. It was absolutely pouring down! That was the year we went to Wembley. Oh, it were so disappointing, but we were a Second Division side so it was a big ask to beat West Ham with Bobby Moore and all them.

We went on a coach from Todd Lane and it was a brilliant atmosphere travelling down. It was just very exciting to be there. We were positioned near the half-way line and Wembley seemed so big compared to Deepdale. Howard Kendall became the youngest player to play in an FA Cup Final that day. I can see all the players now, Dave Wilson, Alex Dawson, Nobby Lawton, Alan Kelly in goal. They played really well and were winning 2-1 at one stage, but they had a good team did West Ham and scored right near the end to win.

We both played for PNE Ladies and played in testimonials for David Wilson, Alan Spavin and George Ross. Those games were on that rubbish training pitch on Lowthorpe Road. You could just about pick your feet up out of that mud. Mind you, all our pitches were like that so it didn't really matter! 'Between us, we played from 1971 to about 1977.'

We travelled all over and I remember travelling to Southampton to play in the quarter final of the FA Cup. We played on Moor Park to start with as we weren't allowed on the Deepdale pitch. The team disbanded after a few years but reformed when Baxi took over. I (Olive) worked at Baxi and in 1995, Bryan Gray asked us to form a team for a match against a team from Chaffoteaux in France, one of Baxi's customers, I think. We weren't a real team, just a side quickly put together from girls that we knew. But afterwards, me and Jo Harwood thought we'd like to carry on and the new PNE Ladies kicked on from there.

I can't remember us ever not supporting North End or being interested in football! Our Dad, Brother, Uncle and Grandparents were all North Enders so that were it. We just enjoy it and have been season ticket holders for most of our lives. It's in your blood, you just go, it's normal. That's it.

Main photo (L to R): Joyce, Olive.

MAVIS PENSWICK

Oh, it was a good day, a good day! Especially winning. The photo was taken before the semi-final against Sheffield Wednesday at Maine Road in Manchester.

We got a Ribble Bus at the old station in the Tithebarn Street area and we were walking towards there when an Evening Post photographer nabbed us. There were just the four of us and then this other lady came up and joined us so that's how the photo came about.

We were all at school, at Lark Hill Convent. That's me on the far left and that's Anne Collinson, and Eileen Sharples, and Dorothy Robinson. I was fourteen then, in 1954. We'd had the scarves embroidered with the players' names and we must've bought the rosettes. That sign had 'Play Up, Sir Tom' on it and was drawn by somebody at school. She was a good artist and she did a lot of drawings in our autograph books of the players, mostly Tommy Finney. She was well practiced at drawing Tommy Finney.

I can't remember much about the game to be honest, but afterwards it was funny. We went on the upstairs of the bus and I had this rattle which you can see in the photo and I was hanging out of the window rattling it and I dropped it! Luckily we were stopped in a queue of traffic coming out of Maine Road and some kind soul picked it up and brought it back on the bus.

'But it was funny because we knew the picture was going to be in the paper that night, so our first instinct when we got off the bus was to get a copy.'

'We must get a paper', we kept saying. There was a little ginnel between the bus station and Lancaster Road, just where the Guild Hall is now, and at the bottom a man was selling papers so we dashed off down there And it was surprising, as we went down to the bus station at Fox Street, the amount of people who said, 'Oh, they're there!' They recognised us from the paper. It must've been with the four of us being together. And then at night we all went to a dance in Walton-le-Dale, a place called Wally's, I think.

Oh yeah, it was a good day all round. I wish I had the energy now. I go to the football now and collapse when I get back.

I've been supporting North End since I was about five years of age. It was a case of I either went to town shopping with me Mother or I went to football with me Dad. Well, you know kids don't like shopping so the best of the two evils was going to the football.

When I went on with my school friends, we used to meet behind the goals on the Town End. Oh, I had many a date from behind those goals. We used to have folk on you know, chant and scream and laugh. In other words, draw attention to ourselves! I used to think that Malcolm Newlands – he was a goalkeeper – oh, I used to think he was lovely. He was my idol, was Malcolm. It was funny that. And I remember the Brindle Brass Band going around chucking the staff in the air. Oh, and singing 'Margie' with the crowd. Oh, Margie, how I'm thinking of you, Margie. That was their signature tune, you might say.

I saw some great players and that was the best of it. Oh yes, I wouldn't have liked to have gone through my life and never been on North End.

PAT MAITLAND

My Mum and Dad always went on the match along with my Uncle Arthur who only lived three doors away. I was roundabout nine when I started going on with them but, soon afterwards, I started going on with my Cousin and some girls from school.

We all went to St Augustine's Roman Catholic school. They used to have this old bell at the school which they would ring for the end of lessons, playtime and all that. Well, it must've been about 1950 and one day at school I asked the nun, well she was the Headmistress, I said, 'Urm, can I borrow the bell please, Mother?'

She said, 'Well, where are you going and what do you want it for?'

I said, 'well, we're going on the Preston North End match and if we score a goal I want to be ringing it.'

It wasn't a great big bell but it was fairly big. Anyway, I got it and me and my friends kept having goes on it all the way up Deepdale Road to the match, and there were loads of fans walking around us. They wouldn't allow it on today would they? Ha!

I continued asking for it after that and sometimes she would say no and other times she'd let us have it. I was only young, and a bit shy, but my friends would say, 'Oh no, I can't ask,' so I'd say, 'Go on then, I'll ask. She can only say "no" can't she?' So that's what we did. The price then was about 9p to go on, then it went up to a shilling!

Of course, Tommy Finney was my favourite but there were some good 'uns though. I mean in different positions. I liked Tommy Docherty. I thought he was good. My Dad liked Charlie Wayman. Oh, he loved Charlie Wayman did my Dad. He used to say, 'Oh, he's good. He just floats it over and he's got nothing to do but put it in!'

'If I didn't get on the match, I used to ask him, 'How did Finney play, Dad?' And he'd say, "Well, not as good as he usually plays but he still had a good'un!"'

I remember we always used to have eggs and bacon on a Saturday night after the match when we came home; that was our ritual. My Mum used to say, 'Get table cloth on, Pat and get some bread buttered!' Then we'd all sit down to eat and discuss the match. I'd ask Dad what he thought and, if we'd got beat, it would always be, 'We shouldn't have got beat by such and such a body' and, 'he should never have scored' and all that kind of stuff. Ha!

It's changed a lot now. I hate the cheating and the diving. You just didn't get it back then. The ground has changed a lot too, of course. I used to love standing on The Paddocks but I prefer to sit these days. And the new cards for getting in are brilliant. But still, I wouldn't be allowed to bring that bell on, would I?

PAUL EASTHAM

My PNE claim to fame after all these years is that me and my family – my two Sons and the Grandchildren – finished up printed on the back of a bus as part of the 'Generation Deepdale' promotional campaign.

My Dad was a fan and he used to take me and my younger Brother on.

'We never even thought of supporting anyone else.'

It was PNE and that was it. We used to watch from the cinder track; all the kids sat there. We'd all be leaping about when they scored. We were in awe of the players.

I remember once, my neighbour took me on. It was Boxing Day and my Dad was working – he worked for Ribble Motors – and we went on the old Kop. Normally, we were Town Enders, and I remember looking about at the crowd and it was swaying to and fro like the sea. It was absolutely packed.

There'd always be constant applause for Tom Finney from The Paddocks whenever he had a run or came back to his position. He was magic. Without a doubt the best player I've ever seen. Incredible, and a very modest man. I remember his last game in 1960 against Luton Town. There was 30,000 people on that day and many of them crying at the end.

Whenever PNE were away, if it were a big match, my Dad would take us to the LEP offices on Fishergate where they did a Stop Press report. There used to be loads of people waiting for those match reports in the Stop Press. It's so different now. Everything is instant. The other day our Granddaughter, Evie, was with us and she kept checking the scores of the Cup matches on her phone and she was like, 'Oh, Preston a goal up!' Then later, 'oh, Hull have

scored!' And I was thinking of the days of the cinder track and on reserves matches when the first team were away.

They used to get huge crowds for the reserves in those days. They used to carry a blackboard around the track when Preston had scored or conceded and you used to know before it reached you what the score was because of the reaction of the crowd. It always seemed to be good news back then too. Oh dear! And now, it's incredible isn't it. Now we get it instantly like Evie with her phone. Amazing.

I can remember watching North End in the 1954 final and the disappointment afterwards but, oh, they had a tremendous homecoming. It was mixed with the hope that we'd be back very soon but that didn't happen, not until the '64 cup run of course.

The game that stands out for me is the semi-final at Villa Park, played in torrential rain. It seems like yesterday. It was hammering down from the moment we set off to the moment we got back. They wouldn't have played today in that rain and mud. It would've been called off I'm sure. Anyway, Villa went a goal up and Dawson equalised with a penalty. Then late on, the ball was cleared from a corner and Singleton, from about forty yards out, booted the ball back. Whether he was really going for goal, I don't know, but we were right behind the goal and just watched it sail into the net. Incredible! I don't think he got many, but that was a great one.

It's a way of life, PNE. If they win, everyone is happy in the family and my neighbour is happy. It means so much to so many. That's what supporting PNE means.

Photo: Margaret and Paul Eastham.

31

TONY SLATER

I got my first season ticket in 1946 and it cost fifteen shillings for the season. I used to walk up Deepdale Road with Bill Shankly and my best mate at school, Tony 'Chang' Singleton.

We were in awe of Shanks and just walked beside him, but we couldn't understand a word he said. I had a season ticket every year until National Service and then every year since, apart from when I lived in Spain.

In 1962 I was one of a group of people who helped form the PNE Supporters Club. We used to meet in the old Pavilion Stand and a committee was formed which included Club Secretary, George Howarth, his assistant, Stuart Webb – who went on to big things with Cloughie at Derby – and Sir Tom.

A separate Ladies committee was also set up which included Brenda Busby and Olive Leeming, the Chairman's wife who was also the mother-in-law of Mike Elwiss. Then it was decided to build a Supporters Club and work began on that in 1963. The building was a tremendous success. It was managed by Alf Dodd, a real authoritarian figure who ran the club with a rod of iron. I used to run all the entertainment and Willie Cunningham would organise old time dancing for me on a Monday night. At one point, we were giving PNE £30,000 a year.

During the reign of Alan Ball Senior, I was asked by then-PNE-reporter, Norman Shakeshaft if I could raise funds to help equip the Mighty Whites with something new called a VCR. Apparently only Manchester City had one at the time so I set about organising and compering a number of fundraising shows at the old Club Royale. For the final show and presentation, I managed to acquire the services of Solomon King who topped the bill. Many will remember Solomon had a worldwide hit with 'She Wears My Ring' in 1968.

After this I did numerous shows to help PNE players and, in 2000, recorded a 7-track CD with our Division Two winning squad to raise money for St Catherine's Hospice and Derian House.

I also worked quite a bit with Sir Tom for his charities. Tom used to let me have signed books and photos which I would auction off at the many fundraising events I organised, but one in particular stands out.

There was a show I arranged in which we were auctioning off a signed Sir Tom Finney shirt. The idea was that Sir Tom would meet us at Deepdale so that a photo could be taken as he presented the shirt in person, but unfortunately our meeting place got mixed-up.

I remember I rang Sir Tom several times to see where he was – there were no mobile phones then – but Sir Tom wasn't answering because he was obviously out at a different meeting place. I told the couple who had won the shirt that we'd have to rearrange the presentation and photo but said I would just try to contact him one last time. Well, this time Sir Tom answered. He explained he thought our meeting place was somewhere else and asked if the couple were still there. When I said they were he immediately got in his car and drove to Deepdale.

Everyone was happy and we got a great photo. For me, it was typical of the great man. He would never decline when asked for help. When he passed away, I was invited to write a piece about him for the LEP's tribute which I was honoured to do. He was a true gentleman with old-school values and I was blessed to have watched him play at Deepdale.

Photo courtesy of Tony Slater. (L to R): Tony Slater, Sir Tom Finney.

2
MEDIA

BILL WHISKER
PROFOUND VALLEY

My Mum and Dad were divorced and, as a kid, Saturday was the day I saw Dad. We went everywhere: museums, stately homes, swimming baths, castles, The Pleasure Beach, Frontier Land, Camelot – everywhere!

Dad was not a football fan but then one Saturday, for whatever reason, he decided we'd go to Deepdale. It changed everything. Shrewsbury were the victims as North End won 6-1 with Micky Conroy scoring a hat-trick. But it wasn't just about the football, which was straight from John Beck's school of alternative science. North End were winning and the Town End was unreal. Drums, trumpets, ticker tape, bog rolls, the biscuit tin guy, the Pink Panther! The noise was deafening and the chants witty and inventive. We were part of something special and were hooked. From then on, we barely missed a home match and away and reserve games soon followed.

A couple of years later in August 1995, my mate, Stanners and I were enjoying a summer's evening in Euxton, hanging around, drinking cheap cider as teenagers did back then. We got talking to an older lad who was a North Ender and he said Steve Wilkinson had moved in round the corner. We didn't really believe him but, emboldened by the Diamond White, marched round and, even though it was half ten at night, started banging on the door. All of a sudden there he was, Stevie Wilkinson, North End's new £100,000 signing stood before us in all his glory. This was our chance to welcome him to Lancashire, get his autograph, let him know what the club meant to the fans and worship our new hero.

'Alright, lads?', he said.

'Err, is Dean in?', Stanners blurted, despite the fact we didn't know anyone called Dean.

'He doesn't live here anymore.', said Wilko, and that was that. We lost our bottle. Off we trotted, happy to have caught a glimpse of one half of the new strike force Gary Peters claimed would guarantee goals.

I've often wondered if Wilko knew we were half-cut teenage PNE fans or actually thought we were looking for someone called Dean. Maybe he'll read this book.

Towards the end of 2016, I started Profound Valley. I felt not enough was being made of our club's history, both its wonderful successes and glorious failures. I wanted to be a positive voice and create a place where North Enders could unite and reminisce.

At the start, I was reluctant to show my face and enjoyed no one knowing who was behind Profound Valley, but that changed when Channel 5 began asking for content for their highlights show. It was weird at first but I do enjoy doing bits for TV. I've also been on BT Sport and Sky Sports talking PNE. Everyone I know has told me they enjoy the content and I've met loads of people through Profound Valley. It's great when people come up to me in the pub or at away games. PNE fans aren't like fans of other clubs. The club means everything to us and when I get talking to people it's amazing how much we've all got in common.

As for the name? Synonyms, cha! Profound meaning deep, and a dale is a valley. It's a funny and silly way of saying Deepdale. I've had it in my head for years without really knowing why. It's esoteric to a point but unique and interesting. Once you get it, you get it. I'm not Profound Valley, I'm Bill. Profound Valley is Deepdale, The Home of Football.

Facebook & Twitter @ProfoundValley
Youtube: Profound Valley
Instagram: profoundvalley

BLACKY

THE NOSEBAG FANZINE

Around the age of six, I actually started supporting Arsenal. This came about with us needing football kits for school and a random Saturday trip to JJB on the corner of Mount Street and Fishergate.

I came out with the cheapest strip on sale, the 1991-1993 Arsenal away kit with the interlocking yellow and blue triangles. My old fella had been a North Ender since the 1950s but by the early 1990s, due to work and family, he only followed them on the radio and via the LEP. Then, on Tuesday 9th March 1993, he decided to initiate me and took me on the old West Stand at Deepdale for a night game. We lost 3-1 to Swansea and it's said I turned to him and asked if it was a real football match. Still, a few weekends later I took it upon myself to slash my Arsenal shirt.

The best era was the late 1990s and early 2000s. Strangely, my favourite memories are of loan players: Eric Meijer geeing up the fans at Watford and Brett Angel's scoring run. But I think our midfield pairing of Gregan and Ranks was absolutely stunning and, for me, Gregan never performed if his sidekick, Rankine wasn't in tow. Whilst not the most gifted, Rankine brought more than just footballing ability.

One game that always warms me from that era was Bristol Rovers away in April 2000. Bristol were flying and, while we weren't doing too bad ourselves, we went as underdogs. We came away with a 2-0 win and from then on nothing was to stop us! This was my first away day on the train. Some of the older North End lads took me under their wing and, as they weren't shy in sharing the beers, it was also perhaps my first experience of underage boozing. That was a Saturday but I love midweek aways the most.

There's something about travelling the length and breadth of the country of an evening to watch the lads under the floodlights. 200 in Gillingham on a Tuesday night is more my style than 3,000 at West Brom on a Saturday.

'I started The Nosebag in 2019.'

I've always been interested in the subculture surrounding fooball and absolutely adore the mid-1990s. I enjoyed the fanzine culture and had written for a few of the old North End ones. I felt it was an art form that was missing with all this social media so I began doing some research in early 2019 and by May decided to give it a bash. For the name, I wanted something totally fresh and different and, in honour of Trev, thought a horse theme appropriate. The Nose Bag is something you can get stuck in to or just chew away at; it's a play on words.

Since I started, I've been more than happy with the response. It's difficult with anything new to get a foot in the door but our readers have been fantastic in giving good reviews and the unofficial North End community are magnificent in the way they've pushed us across social media. The From the Finney podcast even included us in their recommended international break reading. I've come a long way from issue one when I had no PC, no printer, no editing software and no idea!

I work ahead on issues and I'm constantly thinking of articles that could be of interest or receiving new content. It's always a work in progress, with each new publication a battle to be better than the last.

Twitter: @tnbfanzine
Facebook: @tnbfanzine
Website: http://Thenosebag.bigcartel.com

JAKE OATES
FROM THE FINNEY PODCAST

From the Finney just started out as a website. It was myself and Oli – one of my co-hosts on the podcast – who wrote the first content for the site, then Dan, another regular on the podcast, joined us and it's grown from there.

And Jimmy, the manager of the PNE Supporters' Team, regularly joins us for the weekly episodes we record post-match.

'From the Finney Meets . . .' is a monthly episode where I meet with former managers, players or someone connected with the club and we talk about their time at PNE, hear their stories, memories and much more. This began as a written interview series when I interviewed my friend and former left-back, Matt Hill. However, when the podcast took off, I had the idea to take it over to the pod and it's kicked on from there.

I try to get these episodes done in person. It can sometimes take a few weeks or even months to get everything confirmed with a guest, but I've found everyone I've interviewed to be very accommodating. I interviewed Colin Murray, the host of Saturday night's EFL highlights show on Quest TV. To spend the day with him in London at the BBC and Quest studios and talk about North End was superb, and I once got locked in an office building in Liverpool at 9:30pm with Neil Mellor. Luckily, after about five minutes of panicking, we managed to get out.

But my favourite so far has to be Graham Alexander, without a shadow of a doubt. He was a hero of mine growing up and so to have him sitting in my living room for three-and-a-bit hours talking about his career at North End was like a dream come true. He also got in my Wife's good books as he ate more of her homemade shortbread than I did!

We record the weekly episodes every Sunday which involves the recording and editing and then scheduling it for release on a Monday morning. There's no budget and I learnt it all on the job, so to speak, but we seem to be doing okay. We've published over fifty episodes since we put the first one out on May 26th 2019 and have had over 28,000 downloads. We've amassed a decent following on social media and people in places as far-flung as Qatar, Cambodia and China have downloaded the pod which is amazing.

I sit on the Sir Tom Finney stand and have done since I started going to Deepdale regularly as a young boy. Supporting North End runs in the family. My Grandad and Dad are both big fans and it just became a part of my life, quite a big one to be fair. I work in digital marketing and I had the idea to start a website where I could just write my thoughts about North End. My thinking behind the name was that it would be my thoughts from the Finney stand, so to speak, and it just kind of stuck. It's gone down really well on the whole and I just want to continue producing good quality content for the PNE faithful, see continued growth and who knows what will happen? The From the Finney podcast is on all the major streaming platforms.

FB/Insta/Twitter: @fromthefinney
Website: www.fromthefinney.co.uk

Photo courtesy of Jake Oates.

JOHN KELLY

PNE ONLINE

A fan named Wattie created PNE-Online. Over the years this expanded into more of a PNE and Preston community forum and, prior to social media, was really the only unofficial place you could discuss anything PNE on the internet.

When Wattie decided to move on, the site was taken over by a group of longstanding members. Later, I was asked if I would like to become a moderator which, given I spent half my life on there, I was delighted to do so. For much of my time moderating I was also on the committee of a PNE Supporters group, so the two tied in nicely. The forum continued to grow and then one day I was asked to take over as full time administrator.

PNE-Online is non-profit and ad free, and without the commitment of our patrons who contribute to running costs and development, there would be no forum. This is something we are immensely proud of and, whilst we know the forum is not for everyone's tastes, we believe it is one of the best football forums out there. But we are more than just a PNE forum and have a wide range of sections open for debate, including 'General Football', 'Local News' and 'Entertainment'.

'There's nothing that isn't debated. If it's legal, we encourage any topic.'

I've made some great friends through PNE-Online but sadly some are no longer with us. When one of our most popular and controversial users sadly passed, the forum came together. Shaky had been with us for years and for his funeral many members, including some who had never met him, went up to Cumbria in PNE shirts to pay their respects. Shaky was what the forum has always been about: characters. Folk you may have never met, folk you may disagree with passionately. It's a Preston community

like no other. You may hear some detractors, but to me, it's a place where people can come together to have a natter, a rant or even ask for support in our important 'Mental Health' section.

Being part of the Preston community and supporting local charities has always been something we've thrived on. More recently, the forum supported The Big Sleep Out for the Foxton Centre which a few members and I helped to promote and took part in. We worked closely with PNE Community to spread the word and, alongside 300+ attendees, helped to smash the target and raise thousands of pounds for a great cause. We've also played a huge role in helping Gentry Day become what it is today and we will continue to help with fan-led events as we go forward.

In total, we've had over 10,000 registered users, and thousands of 'lurkers' who just view as guests and we recently had our 2.5 millionth post! It's actually possible to view every post, way back to the very first if you so wished! We feel that, by keeping the entire database, we have a historic look of North End over the years, and along with our dedicated volunteer moderators, we hope to be around for many more years to come.

As for me, it was inevitable I would end up supporting North End. My parents even met at the old PNE Supporters Club in what was the old 'Legends' building. We have traced back that someone in our family has been attending Deepdale since the club was formed so at least, at some point, a Kelly has seen us be the best team in the world!

Website: www.pne-online.net
Twitter: @pneonline

MARK INGLIS
PEBBLE LEAGUE

Years ago, when they closed down the BBC 606 forum for individual clubs, my Uncle decided, along with two or three others, to start their own little forum and prediction league.

He was a bit of an IT freak and set up the website as it is now and via ProBoards, who run all the background stuff, they created PEBBLE League.

Then one night a defector, as I would put it, decided he wanted to take his own group out of the forum and pulled all the accounts, blocking everyone from using it. At first my Uncle didn't know what was going on. Anyway, we managed to get it back up and running. I took over the Prediction League, a couple of people said they'd help run the other parts, and it kicked off from there.

'Now we have nearly 800 members, including some regulars, with over 10,000 posts.'

The Prediction League is very popular and I run that in the background. As forums go, PEBBLE is quite small but that also means it's quite friendly. There's not much swearing; we're known as the friendly forum. We've created our own badge for the forum and some of us meet up in Finney's before games.

About five years ago one of our members, The Flying Plumber as he was known, sadly passed away. He was a popular and regular poster so we arranged a meet up and placed a wreath with the letters 'TFP' on the Splash to honour him. I think it meant a lot to his family. The group was a place he visited to chat about North End and he was a very knowledgeable chap. It was nice to remember him and also to meet some of the members.

Some years ago, Iain Hulme was injured for a match and popped up on Twitter commenting on the game so, jokingly, I sent him a link to our forum, as back then we had something called the Shout Box where people could chat during matches. I didn't expect anything but then the next thing, Hulmey signed up and started chatting with our fans about the match! At that time, he had god-like status amongst our fans. It was so funny. All of a sudden there was this hero of ours having a level-headed chat with us. Amazing!

In 2015, I didn't think we were going to get to the Play-off Final, to be honest, and booked a family holiday for the week before. When we reached the final, the forum was chatting away asking who's going to Wembley and I said I'm not as I can't afford it having just been on holiday. Well, the members all chipped in and got me a ticket for the match and coach travel to Wembley! I thought it was amazing. They didn't need to do it. I know it was a 'thank you' for all that had happened with the forum, but still, for me, it was wow!

I was born in Preston but lived in Leicester when I was a kid then moved back up here when I was ten. Me Uncle took me on my first game and we went on the old Paddock. That was 32 years ago, back in the day when it was £2.50 for a ticket! For me, supporting PNE means something to focus on, something to be proud of. I don't want me kids supporting Man United, I want them to have an identity. When people ask where they're from, they can say I'm from Preston and I support Preston North End. It's about identity.

Website:pebbleleague.com
Twitter: @PEBBLELEAGUE
Photos (Top R): Mark Inglis. (Lower): Pebble League members.

PETE PADDOCK

PRESTON NORTH END FANS FORUM

It's a strange one for me because when I was younger, I was more for following Man United and Liverpool like everyone at school, but my Dad was a North Ender and a plumber so you can imagine who his idol was!

He used to say, 'Why don't you go on North End?' but he didn't drive and he never took me then, one day, one of our neighbours asked if I'd like to go. I remember Alan Spavin was playing that day and then years later, when John McGrath was manager, I started going on a bit more, but I only really decided late on that I was supporting PNE, and funny enough it was when the two guys both scored a hat-trick against Mansfield. You know the game I'm on about! I thought, you know what, I'm gonna come every week.

'Deep down, I always knew I was a North Ender. My Grandad was a North End fan and my Dad and his Brothers, so it was instilled in me.'

But that double hat-trick, Saville and Wilkinson, that did it. I got a season ticket not long after that!

I can still remember the smell of the old ground, the pies, and everything else! It was all standing then and I do miss a bit of that. I'd still stand now to be fair. I used to go on the Kop and occasionally the Paddock as well and, if you remember, you could walk from one stand to another in those days.

A group of us once went to Bristol in a limousine for the last day of the season under Moysie. It worked out cheaper for six of us to hire a limo than go on the train or the coach!

I remember we went in a pub and all these Bristol City fans welcomed us then of course we won the match 2-0. That was in 2000, the year we won promotion under Moysie.

With the forum, I wanted to do something different because a lot of friends were asking me to stop putting North End stuff on my Facebook page, so I thought I'd start a group and see how it goes – that was in 2012.

I got Alfie Hornby and Matt Hill and I was trying to see how many people I could get on it. Eventually I had to get other admins involved because I'm working all the time and we'd grown so much. Then around 2015 we restructured and I brought some new people in. Stephanie runs the Twitter page for us now and that's doing well. Sometimes I can come home late from work and find my inbox is full but I do love it! Yes, we get some negatives, but one of the rules is that everyone can voice their opinion, and if people disagree, just please don't get nasty.

We try and support different causes too. We started the 'Legend' wreath for Sir Tom along with Daz Livesey who has since sadly passed. We took the wreath around the ground and then laid it down. Granada Reports was there and a lot of fans talked about what Sir Tom meant to them. It was great to be a part of it, and then Daz took it forward each year after that.

This forum means a lot to me because I like people to have their say, plus you can learn a lot from other people's comments. As for PNE, they mean the world to me now. North End, that's all I think about, but it took me a while!

www.facebook.com/groups/PrestonNorthEndFansForum

1982-83 match-worn shirt.
Courtesy of Jonny Richardson.

TERRACE
TALK

ANDREW WILSON

I love Deepdale. I know I'm biased but I do think it's one of the best grounds in the country. The new stands aren't straight out of a flat pack identikit, and to me it still feels like the old place when I'm there.

I sit on the Alan Kelly Town End these days but started off on the old Kop. I can still see that yellow wall and the wooden steps at the back.

'I wouldn't say I didn't have a choice in following North End as my Dad wasn't a fan, but he did take me on my first ever game – a 4-1 victory at home to Reading.'

It was during the 70-71 season and Gerry Ingram scored a hat-trick. It was the only game I saw of that promotion campaign but it wasn't a bad start! I haven't got many items of North End memorabilia. Like most people, there's a piece of plastic pitch somewhere but I do have a programme from that first match from my mate Kirky which I got framed.

We used to live near the White Hart pub in Fulwood and I could see the floodlights from our house. I went to school at Holme Slack and, when Hugh McIlmoyle signed for North End from Middlesbrough in the 71-72 season, he moved into our road and his sons came to our school. That season, I pestered my parents so much that they allowed me to go on the games on my own. I stood on the windy corner at first. A few years later my Brother, Rog started coming with me and we stood near the tunnel with one of my Mum's friends, Mavis, and her son, Terry (Brooks) who is still a fan today.

I went to a few away games when I was still at school, ones like Bury and Wrexham and the infamous 'Tranmere linesman' Friday night match. Once I left school I started going home and away in earnest, and our slide down the divisions meant lots of us were able to visit different grounds. The re-election season is often mentioned as a low point, but even so, there were good memories – celebrating a win at Mansfield like it was at Old Trafford, and the trip to Torquay in February! Beforehand, we were 91st and 92nd respectively and that dismal defeat saw us dumped at the bottom. I remember we left Preston at 3am straight from the Warehouse and were in Torquay early, and then spent the night in our minibus in a pub car park before the long journey back home on the Sunday! I actually have a fondness for a lot of the re-election team; it kind of wasn't their fault. The club had been in decline for a few years and the late John McGrath is probably my favourite ever manager for rescuing us from all that. He built a new team almost from scratch. It was a great season. John McGrath, an alchemist and a genius.

I've thousands of favourite memories: Alex Bruce's legendary goal at Ewood, the Tony Ellis hat-trick at Bloomfield, Ricardo beating Burnley seemingly on his own, Brian Mooney turning opponents inside out on plastic and grass, Frank Worthington v Wolves, Rocket Ronnie, the Birmingham and Torquay play-off nights, and more recently Wembley, Beckford's second and North End's third, Welsh's tackle, Joey's fist pump.

These days, I'm still a season ticket holder but don't get to as many away games as I'd like but enjoy them when I can. Here's to the future. Come on you Whites!

ARUN PATEL

My Dad came here around 1962 and wasn't into football, only cricket. Back then, you didn't have to be coloured to get into trouble and Dad always worried about the violence associated with football.

One day I came home and said, 'Dad, is there any chance I can go and watch PNE?' and he said, 'No, never!' He'd seen fans fighting once on the train station and was worried I might get caught up in it. Then one day in school, someone mentioned PNE had gone up to League Two and were having a celebration at the Cenotaph. It was the 1977-78 promotion season. I pleaded with Dad to let me go and finally he said okay.

The whole of the flag market was packed with North End fans! My Dad, Brother and I sat on the windowsills of the shops on Cheapside, away from the crowd. The players were high up on the steps of the library, and the fans were jumping up and down and singing.

'I was in awe. I was ten years old and it was the first time I'd witnessed a big crowd, a football crowd. I was over-whelmed.'

Then one of my teachers from school – I think her name was Mrs Peacock – walked past and I said hello. She looked, stopped, then looked again, then walked back to my Dad and said to him, 'I'm very surprised.' Well, back at school I was full of it. In front of the whole class Mrs Peacock asked me what I'd been doing there and I was so proud.

For me, back then, it was like, *that's it, it's gotta be Preston North End!* And I remember for P.E. at school my Mum bought me a white t-shirt with a blue collar and

triangle from Merigold's Sports shop and I told everyone it was a PNE shirt, but I still wasn't allowed to go on Deepdale!

Years later, in the 82-83 season, my mate, Shaun said we were playing Blackpool in the cup. He said we've got to be careful, there'll be fighting afterwards in the car park but it didn't put me off. I thought, *I'm going to that match!* It was my first match and we won 2-1. I sneaked on, told Dad I was going to town. I was on the Kop and there were all these rocker types. Ah, the days of mods and rockers.

Once I left school, I started to go on all the time. In those days the Kop would start jumping up and down shouting, 'We all hate Blackpool, we all hate Blackpool!' It would go all around the ground like a wave, everyone singing for a good five minutes. Brilliant!

Remember Torquay at home when Moore got sent off for throwing a punch? The last match on plastic – that was something! My family used to have a shop on Inkerman Street and I worked there from the age of 17 to 47. The morning after the game, I went to open up at 6am and there were pieces of plastic pitch scattered all over the street. I thought, *what the hell is going on?* Then outside the shop was a massive piece so I took it inside and I've kept it ever since!

I also have a piece of carpet from the Director's Lounge from when they knocked down the old Pavilion stand. Somebody left it at the shop with my Brother and said, 'Oh, give that to Arun for me.' Ha. To this day I still don't know who brought it!

BARRY DAWSON

For Wembley in 2015, we got the return train from Manchester to London at £50 each and actually managed to upgrade to First Class for an extra £15. Then after we'd won, I went to the Marks & Spencer just outside Euston and bought us a bottle of champagne.

I don't drink, but we'd won and we had to celebrate, so there we were drinking champagne in First Class!

It was just an amazing day. Before kick-off, we walked all the way around the stadium, and then who did we see but Roop on his bike! We'd met him before at Preston and he spotted Jack and said, 'Eh, Jack!' and came running over. We then got a load of pictures. Oh, it was brilliant. We had flags, scarves, the jester hats, everything. That whole day is my favourite PNE memory, alongside beating Chesterfield at home. Beckford's wonder goal was unreal. The crowd went mad, and Jack remembers seeing a guy do the worm onto the pitch at the end when we all ran on!

'I actually went to school with Paul McKenna and he was an outstanding sportsman, even then. We were good friends and, although we left school and went our separate ways, I always followed his career with interest.'

Then a year ago, I met him for the first time in 25 years when his son was playing my son at football. When he saw me, he came running over to me. 'Alright Baz? It's Paul!' I said, 'Flippin' 'eck!' And then afterwards he actually asked my lad if he'd play for his club, which is Eccleston. It was mad.

We're members of a local bowling club and some old boys go in there to play bowls. They're all North End fans and in the days of Tom Finney they used to take the train from Southport to Preston then walk up to Deepdale. They live in a home opposite the club and sadly aren't really fit or healthy enough to come to Deepdale now. Anyway, I got a shirt from the club shop and all the players signed it and we got it framed and hung it up in the club. Tom Clarke wrote on it 'To Tarleton Bowling Club, love Preston North End.' It was brilliant by the club and players, and when the old boys come in and see it, it's very touching.

One year, just before Christmas, 2017 I think, we were asked by friends to join them in a box at Deepdale for a match against Forest. Anyway, we were having a meal when Trevor Hemmings walked into the room and wished us all a happy Christmas. We were flabbergasted, and he gave us all a scarf as a present! Yeah, Mr Hemmings gave us all a scarf, and now I wear it every time I come. So that was a shock, the owner walking in.

When we're going to watch North End, it's all about family, spending time with my Son, bonding together. We always go on the matches together as a family when we can – my Uncle Jim, Son, Jack and his mate, Lewis. I think it's in yer. It's the same as any club, you just love it. It's a good family club, very well-run, it really is. They do a lot for kids and the older folk too, they try to help them in anyway – it's brilliant.

Photo (L to R): Jack Dawson, Barry Dawson, Jim Scambler.

BEV TAYLOR

On the match a few years ago I noticed the big screen advertising about Simon Grayson doing a bike ride for Prostate Cancer UK. Now, I love doing anything for charity, and I love doing anything for Preston North End, so I was very interested.

A few nights later, I dragged my friend, Rachel, along to a promotional evening at the Bull & Royal. Mark Lawrenson and Simon Grayson were there and, with a team from Prostate Cancer UK, they explained they were looking for people in our area to join up for the 'Football to Amsterdam' bike ride in aid of the charity. They were after fans from different clubs to cycle the 140-odd miles from Barnsley to the Ajax stadium in Amsterdam. Easy, or so I thought!

We contacted the club and they kindly donated two PNE shirts for Rachel and me to wear on the journey, and so in the summer of 2017, we cycled to Amsterdam and raised £2,500. The next year I invited/dragged another friend to join us and we had proper shirts made and got local companies to sponsor us. That year, Belinda, Rachel and I raised £1,500. It was an amazing experience and great fun meeting all the different footy fans. However, I didn't do it this year and I'm gutted because Jon Parkin was doing it and I'm a big PNE autograph hunter.

When I turned fifty, I retired and quickly became bored. I'd been playing goalkeeper in hockey for a long time at work and suddenly stopped, but then I saw an advert for walking football. I thought, well, I'm not a footballer, but if they need a goalkeeper I might see if I can get myself in nets.

I joined up and later was lucky to win Player of the Tournament in a walking football competition in Portugal. There were forty teams and I was the only female but it wasn't a token gesture, honest! I was part of the PNE Women's Walking Footballers who got to the final of the FA People's Cup. The final was down at St George's where, unfortunately, we got beat 1-0 by Birmingham.

It was the first time they'd ever had women's walking football in the People's Cup so it would've been great if we'd won it, but I've now got a nice FA People's Cup medal, even if it is a losers medal.

It's a great feeling wearing the PNE badge for the walking teams. I was brought up on Deepdale Road and more or less lived opposite the ground which explains why I'm a massive fan. My earliest PNE memory is of seeing Alex Bruce scoring and, over the years, I've loved watching players like Gareth Ainsworth and Grezza. For me, my favourite players have always been the ones who show some passion, those who put the shirt on and make that connection with us in the stands.

(L to R): Rachael Carroll, Bev Taylor.

CHRISTIAN WAINMAN

Many years ago my Sister, Melissa, played for PNE Ladies under twelves where my Dad, Steve, was the coach. As I got older, I became more interested in football and Dad would take me along to watch the games.

Then in 2000, the under twelves held a fundraiser event at Deepdale and as soon as I entered the ground I was hooked! At the event, I was lucky enough to win the raffle and was presented with the prize at PNE's next home game. That Saturday, I was wheeled onto the pitch and received a shirt signed by David Lucas. It was my first ever match at Deepdale, and I've only missed nine home games since!

'I have some great memories from following North End. In April 2007 we booked a hotel room for the Coventry v PNE game. As we parked the car, we saw John Sumner walking across the car park and realised the PNE squad were staying there too. It was a brilliant time.'

The players took me to their hearts and made sure I had a weekend to remember, particularly when the fire alarm went off in the middle of the night and Paul Simpson said I'd done it on purpose so I could see the lads again!

Another lasting memory for me is my 21st birthday in November 2013. It actually fell on a home match and the stewards surprised me with a little party at the entrance to the food area in the Sir Tom Finney Stand. My friends had a collection for me and then Glyn Snodin walked over and gave me a signed shirt! It was an amazing day. We got the shirt framed and it now hangs proudly on my bedroom wall.

I also have a shirt from Claude Davis which he gave to me at the end of the PNE v Cardiff game in 2005. At that time, Craig Brown had organised a number of open days behind the Alan Kelly Stand. They had tables on the concourse and the players took it in turns to speak to the fans, sign autographs and hand out photos. Claude knew my Sister and she told him I was a fan and where we sat. He spotted us at the end of the game and came over. I had no idea it was going to happen!

My Dad takes me to the games and we've had season tickets for about fifteen years now. We don't go to many away games due to poor viewing facilities at some grounds but of the ones I've been to, Aston Villa and Wolves are my favourites, and Wembley of course!

Over the years, I've got to know a lot of the older players like Ricardo Fuller, Richard Cresswell and Sean St Leger, and I've made many friends through supporting PNE. Football is a major part of my life I just love it.

CHRISTINE SCHOFIELD

PNE has always been a part of my life. My Dad, Colin Aspinall, was a big North End fan and his hero was Sir Tom. Dad was a typewriter engineer for Preston Typewriters and they looked after the typewriters of the Finney business, so he knew Sir Tom quite well.

He was also a big fan of Bill Shankly. Some of my earliest memories are of Dad taking me on the game, lifting me over the turnstiles and sitting me on the barriers at the front of the Kop. My Uncle Jim also came with us and brought his dad, Mr Fawcett, who lived next door but one to us on St Paul's Road. Mr Fawcett was blind and Dad and Uncle Jim would describe the game to him and tell him what was happening. I remember once everyone around us joining in and Mr Fawcett saying, 'They are all helpful, but I think they're all watching different games!' Back then Alan Spavin was one of my favourites, but my all-time favourite is Ricky Heppolette.

My Mum, Joyce, said when they were children, she and Dad were neighbours on Great Hanover Street and apparently he used to pinch her ball and hair ribbons. They got married in 1956. Mum used to say he proposed on North End and Dad always chipped in, 'Not during the match, I waited until half-time – I didn't want to miss anything!' Mum couldn't remember the score, she was too excited, but Dad said we won!

She used to go on the games with him up until the children started arriving, when I think money must've been tight. Dad's last game was the 3rd March 2018 against Hull. We had a box for the match and we won 2-1. Due to ill health he didn't go on much for the last few years of his life. Sadly, we lost Dad in the month of June and then Mum in September. After the funerals we took their flowers and left them at Sir Tom's fountain.

I still go on North End and have always taken my boys, Pete and Russ, with me. As new-born babies, they were both driven past Deepdale on their ways home from hospital and are die hard North Enders.

They have lots of happy PNE memories: queuing up at midnight to buy new kits, ripping up parts of the pitch after the last game on plastic, playing on Deepdale in school boy finals, seeing the mural above the seats on the old Pavilion, singing We Are the Champions on the pitch when we got promoted as Division 3 champions . . . so many memories.

'Russ, our youngest Son, was the mascot in 1995 for the 3-2 win over Fulham when David Beckham scored from a free-kick. And now we are making new memories with our Grandson, Ryan, who was a mascot in December 2017.'

We have been there when struggling for re-election to celebrating promotions. PNE is just part of our DNA. It has been there from us being born and I can't ever imagine it not being there. It's who we identify with.

Photo, L to R, Back: Russ Schofield, Christine Schofield, Pete Schofield. Front: Ryan Schofield, Katie Schofield.

DALE JAY

It was only really in my first two years of high school when I became a North End fan. My Grandad always kept me up to date with North End but neither of my parents was ever really interested in football.

A few of my friends at school had season tickets with their families so we all decided to get one together in the 2004-2005 season. Every home game, we'd meet up about 11am and get the train from Leyland. We'd walk from the station up to the ground, get fish and chips from Ali's on Meadow Street, and then head to the museum for an hour or so. We made a day out of it every week and those early memories will stay with me forever.

My first match was actually Burnley away in 2003/2004. Alexander scored a penalty that day and Fuller got sent off. Before he headed down the tunnel, Fuller walked over to the away end to clap us all.

'The atmosphere was electric – it was an amazing day. I remember travelling on the coach and being really excited. That was really the beginning of my PNE journey, a cold but bright day in east Lancs.'

In 2004/2005 we had tickets for Plymouth away. It was a Saturday 3pm kick-off so it was an early start. Our plan was to wake about 5:30am and walk to Tesco in Leyland where the coach was setting off but, unfortunately, we slept through the alarms and I remember waking to the sound of my Mum saying, 'It's 6:25!' The coach was setting off at half-past.

We all looked at each other, jumped up and got ready as quick as we could. Mum was already in the car with the engine running. She was a childminder at the time so there was a baby seat in the back which one of my friends sat in. By the time we got to Tesco we'd missed the coach.

The following season, the fixture was midweek and we took the day off school to go down. It was a freezing cold day in January and the game was called off the moment we arrived. A 600-mile round trip for nothing, but nevertheless we decided to go again a few weeks later for the rearranged fixture. Once more it was a midweek trip and I must say, probably the worst game of football I've ever watched; a 0-0 draw with one shot (off target). Needless to say, we've never gone to Plymouth away since!

Me and my friends from school, Adam and Alex, still get our season tickets together and we still go on away games together when we can. These days we'll look to drive depending on how far it is, and if it's a bit of a journey we might look to stay over. West Ham at Upton Park in 2004/2005 is a stand-out away trip for me. We were right behind the goal and we won 2-1. It was our first London trip for a game and I also had my first Chicken Balti pie!

For me, like many, PNE is not just about football. It's a reason to get out of bed on a Saturday. It's something to look forward to all week. It's about catching up with friends and seeing regular faces on the Alan Kelly, being able to sing in public and cheering on the lads. It's staying to the final whistle win, lose or draw. It's turning up regardless of the weather to support your team and follow them up and down the country. It's the hope that, one day, we will play in the Premier League. I love this football club.

DANIEL DUCKWORTH

I'm born and bred Preston and have always supported North End. My Uncle – who's actually a Newcastle United fan – used to bring me on PNE when I was young as my Mum and Dad aren't really into football.

I went on a lot when I was at primary school. Although I can't remember what year I first went, I can remember the old Pavilion stand with its mural and seeing Carlo Nash playing in goal.

One very early memory is of watching PNE play West Ham in the 2005 Play-Off Final. I was in The Sherwood pub; it was heaving and I was sat right at the front. I remember there was a story going around about a lucky Buddha or something. It had become a lucky charm that somebody was taking to all the games, but sadly it didn't work for that match!

My Grandad was a massive North Ender, and we actually scattered his ashes where the goal line is at the Town End. It was his final request. He saw all the greats play. One of those, George Ross, used to deliver my prescriptions! He worked for Broadway Pharmacy and we'd always have a good chat about football; he was a lovely man and PNE through and through. It was sad when he passed, and Sir Tom too.

'On the day of Sir Tom's funeral I skipped university. I said I'm not going in, I have to pay my respects. I was adamant about that.'

I stood at the side of Moor Park Avenue and then went into the stadium and shed a tear along with everyone else. Then we had the match against Leyton Orient where all the players wore 'Finney' on the back of their shirts. I was sat right behind the dugout for that match.

These days I sit on the Finney, almost direct with the centre line. I'm not superstitious but I do have my match day routine. I always set off for the ground at the same time and I always have a Full English for breakfast. I love away games, especially the derbies, but I haven't been to as many as I'd like.

The best away I ever went to was Sheffield United in the FA Cup replay in 2015. That was a good game. We won 3-1 and got Man United in the next round!

The best goal I've ever seen has to be the Joe Garner one against Rotherham. It was sublime. I was actually in hospitality for that game and I remember coming out and we'd just started the second half and, oh, it was a flyer! I could watch it over and over. It was a special moment. When I look back, I think it was a good thing we'd got relegated in 2011. Of course, we were all disappointed at the time but, with hindsight, going down and having to re-build, yeah, it was a good thing overall and we're in good shape now.

Supporting PNE means everything to me – it's a religion. Like I said, I'm from Preston and I'm very proud to be from Preston. Following your local club is just an amazing feeling.

EMMA PRICE

Why do I support North End? A bit of a cliché but it runs in the family as they're our hometown club. I remember Deepdale Duck visiting my primary school to encourage us to attend Deepdale so I went home begging my Dad to take me to a game and, of course, he obliged.

Wembley 2015 is one of the stand-out games for me for obvious reasons but, other than that, it is really difficult to pick just one game. I think one of the reasons I enjoy going to football matches, especially away days, is for the atmosphere and the day out, sometimes more than the football itself. So, for that reason, my favourite games are Fulham away in 2017 when it was Gentry Day and Blackburn in 2016.

'Gentry Day is such a special part of being a Preston fan, and to have hundreds of North End fans dressed to the nines with their bowler hats and singing through London was such a brilliant day.'

Rovers in 2016 was another good day out with 7,000 North Enders making an electric atmosphere. Even better, we sealed the day off with a win.

Joe Garner has to be my favourite ever player for Preston. He's in good company with Graham Alexander, Sean St Ledger, Paul Gallagher and Ben Pearson, but Garner just edges it. I think it was because he played for Preston as a fan and loved every second on the pitch.

The goal he scored against Rotherham was the best goal I've ever had the privilege to see live. Joe also had the pleasure of walking out to a game with my Brother, Matt as the mascot.

The club have been an integral part of our family life and I think they do a lot of fantastic work in the community. In December 2017 I nominated Matt for a PNE 'Whites Christmas' surprise and Declan Rudd and Daniel Johnson shocked Matt and my Sister, Meg by turning up on our doorstep.

Matt is an incredible young man. He was born with a half-working heart, has had three open-heart surgeries and many smaller investigations, but it hasn't stopped him. He is amazing and an inspiration to every person he meets. The players presented Matt with a signed football, and the video of him opening the door is one I think everyone should watch. It is something that will stay with my family and I for the rest of our lives.

Supporting PNE has given me so many good memories, and I genuinely don't know what non-football fans do with their time! I'm a proper geeky fan and love reading up on all the stats and going to the fan forums. I couldn't ever imagine not going to the games and boring everyone stupid talking about PNE all the time.

Photo (L to R): Megan Price, Emma Price, Matthew Price.

GARY JOHNSON

When I was young, some friends started taking me on Deepdale with them and that's how I began. My first game was in 1970 when I was aged eight. I sat in front of the old West Stand at the edge of the pitch on the cinder path with all the other kids.

It was November and freezing. We were chucking the cinders onto the pitch when my mate threw one of my shoes on. I ran on to get it and the next thing I knew a policeman had grabbed hold of me. 'You're not allowed on the pitch, son!' He shouted, 'we'll chuck you out next time that happens!' Ha! It wasn't a great start.

I went on all the time after that. We'd usually go on after half-time for free as we had no money. Sneak up to the side door to get on. Alan Kelly was playing, Alex Bruce and Mark Lawrenson. I can remember when they sold Lawrenson to Brighton.

'So many matches stand out, good and bad.'

New Year's Day 1995 we beat Cardiff 5-0 at home. What a match! Fantastic spirit in the ground. Home games are brilliant during the festive season when everyone has had a few beers. I think Saville scored two that day.

I went to the Wycombe match at Wembley when we lost 4-2. Oh, those play-offs!

On the 28th May 2001, I went to Cardiff with the family to watch the Bolton final. We stopped at Shrewsbury overnight and the next day, after breakfast at The Little Chef, drove down the A49; it was quicker than the motorway. Along the way, we came to stop at a railway junction and, as the train roared past, we could see all the PNE scarves flowing out of the carriage windows. It was amazing to see.

The cars were the same too. Horns beeping, flags and scarves hanging out and people waving. There was a great atmosphere at that match, really good. Even after we'd lost it was still good. I remember walking back and chatting with some Bolton fans who were trying to be kind, saying, 'Unlucky, you'll get there next time', but I was gutted.

Then I was back at Cardiff in 2005 for the West Ham game. We missed a chance and they went up the other end to score with a scuffed shot. It was heartbreaking!

But the best ever for me is the Birmingham play-off semi in 2001. When Rankine scored, everyone went ballistic! I'll never forget that goal. I was on the Kop right behind the goals for the penalties. They had the penalties at the Kop End because the Town End was being rebuilt. They said, 'Don't go on the pitch' and everyone ran on the pitch. It all happened in that match.

Even better was that, later, I took the fun out of Jasper Carrott at a Phil Cool gig in Chipping. My Dad was good mates with Phil and Phil and Jasper used to tour together. I said to him, 'You left your box of champagne behind at Deepdale didn't you, Jasper?' He said, 'Yeah I did. I couldn't believe it. We thought we were home and dry!' They'd brought a box of champagne with them to celebrate but then it was left in the dressing room afterwards, untouched. That was funny that one!

Photo: Gary with grandson, Jayden.

IAN McCULLOCH

There was a game in January 2007 when PNE played Stoke City at Deepdale. Dave Harold, who was another 'top sixteen' snooker player and my roommate on tour, is a mad Stoke fan.

He would come up for the weekend whenever the teams met at Deepdale and I'd go to Stoke for the return fixture, if the snooker calendar permitted.

Dave used to like striking up these elaborate bets and, with each match, they'd get more and more extravagant. The bets always built up a head of steam in the week leading up to the game and would be set in stone over breakfast on the day of the match. One rule was that the away team always got the draw in their favour.

After just seven minutes, Stoke were 2-0 up and I was in shreds, not only for the bet but I was also getting verbally rinsed off Dave! It was still 2-0 at half-time and, as usual, Dave started making all sorts of sub bets attached to the main bet. All good fun but not when you're on the losing end.

So the second half started and things were looking bleak until Paul McKenna scored with 25 minutes to go to give me a bit of hope. I actually used to have a few frames of snooker every week with Paul who wasn't a bad player and could make the odd fifty plus break. Anyway, then Nugent scored with about fifteen minutes left but David still had the draw running in his favour due to Stoke being the away side. The verbals were reaching a crescendo as the final seconds of the match were fading away until, from nowhere, Kelvin Wilson scored with one of the last kicks of the game.

It's fair to say, that evening's meal, and the rather expensive bottle of wine later, tasted very very nice, and didn't cost me a penny.

One incident that put a lump in my throat was at the 2005 Play-Off final in Cardiff. I was doing some work for Sky Sports on the match, which suited me down to the ground, and I went on the Sunday afternoon to meet some friends who were Sheffield Wednesday fans. Wednesday won their play-off final and we went for one or two drinks! It's fair to say, the morning after, I wasn't at my best but I made my way down to the Millennium Stadium to do some work. From memory, it was a piping hot day and not the best weather to be nursing a hangover. I know the Cardiff layout quite well due to playing snooker down there and had arranged to meet a friend of mine, Paul McCullough (no relation) for lunch before the game. Anyone who was there will remember how packed the streets around the ground were and, as I was on the phone to Paul trying to locate him, one girl shouted, 'OMG, it's Ian McCulloch.'

I'd just had fifteen days on the BBC on my run to the Snooker World Championship semi-finals and the media exposure was, and is, huge for that event.

'Suddenly, the girl started singing, 'There's only one Ian McCulloch.' which, at first, was quite embarrassing.'

Next, the group she was with all joined in, then another group joined, and in no time the whole street, maybe a couple of thousand people, were all singing my name. I filled up a bit and started putting my hands up trying to stop them and they all cheered. Amidst all this I still hadn't found Paul, and then we spotted each other about ten feet apart. He was just stood there shaking his head in disbelief. It was a very humbling experience for sure and one I'll never forget!

JACOB BAKER

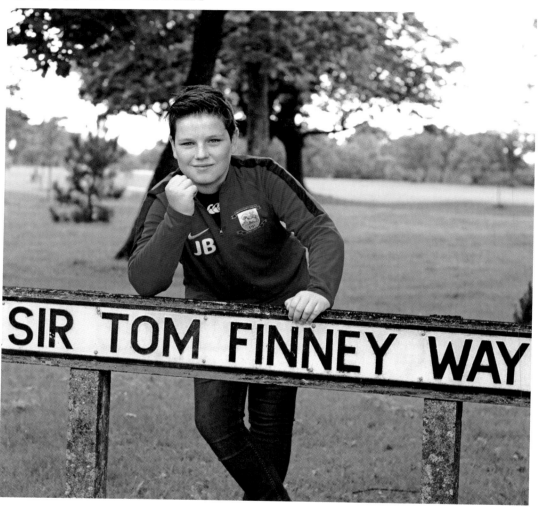

Both my Grandad and Brother support PNE and I started going to games with them. The first match I can remember is a 1-0 win over Rochdale when we sat at the top of the Sir Tom Finney stand. I was aged about seven and have been a season ticket holder ever since.

My favourite PNE memories are of two key moments in the club's recent history. First is Jermain Beckford's goal from the halfway line in the win over Chesterfield in the Play-Off Semi Final. And second is beating Swindon 4-0 in the Final at Wembley.

I travelled to Wembley with my Grandad, Dad and elder Brother on one of the coaches organised by the club. The atmosphere surrounding North End, Preston and then Wembley was surreal, and the stadium defied belief with its daunting appearance.

I remember during the match, I went to the toilet just before half-time in order to beat the rush. I was in the toilets when I heard a massive roar from the East End. Jermaine Beckford had scored and I missed it! But it was a fantastic day and getting promoted to the Championship was brilliant.

I've met a couple of PNE players and one day met Alan Browne in Sainsbury's. I was helping with a fundraiser with the Air Cadets when Alan walked over and made a donation. I asked him if he was Alan Browne, he said he was and that he hoped we could keep going through the festive period and go on to gain promotion.

I was also once lucky enough to be a mascot for North End and I had the pleasure of walking out onto the pitch with then goalkeeper, Chris Maxwell. I was a bit nervous so I tried to make conversation by asking Chris if he watched football on Channel 5. He then replied along the the lines of, 'Only to see my beautiful face!' I still can't suppress a smirk over that comment, even today.

I have a framed photo from that day of me walking out with Chris Maxwell which also includes Tom Clarke and Jordan Hugill.

Another prized North End item I have is a 1996 Third Division Winners scarf. It was my Grandad's and he lets me use it. Both my Grandads are fantastic!

Tom Barkhuizen is my current favourite player. The way his runs, passing and ability leave defences terrified is inspiring.

'For me, supporting PNE is not only a pastime, but a passion. There is truly no better experience than a cold floodlit Deepdale on a rainy Tuesday night.'

The atmosphere is unbeatable with tackles flying in and shots forcing goalkeepers into magnificent saves. Following PNE is to be immersed into a nail-biting world of goals, cards and excitement, unless it's a nil-nil draw, but every team has them. Ha! I love watching PNE; they play a huge part in my life and give me hope and ambition.

JANICE FALCONER

I was born a White. It's in the blood. My Mum, Grandparents, Aunts and Uncles, all PNE fans, and I've brought my children up the same.

My middle child, Christine actually had the honour of being PNE's first ever female ball boy, or I should say, ball girl. Christine was born on Christmas Eve and for her birthday in 1979 I arranged for her to be a ball girl for the following Boxing Day match at Deepdale. She was thrilled and so proud. We were all proud. It was a special day. We beat Shrewsbury Town 3-0 and I have a lovely picture of her which I treasure to this day.

My earliest memories of North End are of walking up Deepdale Road with my Grandad who lived just two minutes away from the long-time PNE mascot, Bobby Roe. We would stop off at my Aunty Eva's house opposite the old Infirmary on the way to the ground. Her family shared a house with PNE player, Bobbie Beattie, and we used to walk to the match with him. My Aunty lived upstairs and Bobbie and his wife, Mary, downstairs.

When I left school, I went to work in an office down Guild Hall Street. At dinner time we'd always go to Joe Dunn's café on Cannon Street and we'd often see Alan Kelly Senior, Les Dagger, John Wylie and Garbutt Richardson in there. In the late 70s and early 80s, we used to run our own coaches to away games. Craven's Coaches they were, sometimes half full, sometimes chock-a-block.

There are plenty of funny stories. When Nobby Stiles and Alan Kelly were in charge we had collections on the bus which we gave to the players for their fish and chips suppers on their way home. One time, I cooked them hot dogs on the coach steps. We also got the players Easter eggs from Thorntons with their names on and donated a huge white bear to Nobby for a coach mascot, but I heard the bear did a bunk when the Doc took over. Apparently he took it for his granddaughter.

I'm keen on crafts and craft fairs and make up bags of mixed sweets and lots of Christmas novelties and gifts, sometimes with a PNE theme. I promote these to my PNE friends who are very supportive. I also have good connections with some players who often donate football kits or memorabilia which I then sell or raffle off.

All my profits are donated to the Rosemere Foundation. The PNE players are very generous as they know it's for a good cause. At a club like ours, it's easy to meet and speak to the lads and it's great to get their autographs and take photos.

My all-time favourite player is Graham Alexander. Remember the Birmingham play-off at Deepdale? Grezza missed a penalty in that match but then redeemed himself by scoring in the penalty shoot-out. I actually have a fish called Grezza, and I have others. One called Gally, one Pearson, and one Preston!

'Supporting North End and following the team has taken me to different places all over the country. It's my social life, and I have some great memories.'

Preston North End is like an extension to my family; we're all Whites together.

Photo: L to R: Christine Falconer, Janice Falconer.

JOHN DEVEY

Supporting PNE? It's historic. My Dad supports them, his Dad supported them, and so on.

Dad used to take us on the old West Stand. We weren't Junior Whites but we used to sit next to where they were seated.

My first North End memory is the last game of the 87/88 season – a 1-2 loss at home to Notts County. I was just in awe at all these blokes around me who seemed to be so mad, and I remember Dad saying, 'Just ignore the swearing and don't tell your Mum.'

On the 27th April 1996, the week of my 14th birthday, we went to Hartlepool United. Just me and Dad had managed to get tickets but Dad wanted a drink so Mum agreed to drive us there. Dad had got the tickets off Kevin 'Killer' Kilbane as he used to be Kev's teacher at school.

'We'd secured promotion the week before at Leyton Orient so there was a real party atmosphere, and just before the final whistle, you could sense the excitement for a good old pitch invasion.'

The final whistle came and we ran onto the pitch to embrace the players. Kev hugged my Dad and I gave him Dad's 1960s PNE scarf. All the way home we sang 'Cheer Up, Gary Peters'. It was a great feeling. Then the following week my Dad went round to Kev's Mum's house to get tickets for the Exeter game and got his scarf back.

Last year, my now-ten-ear-old Daughter went on her first ever home game having refused until then. It was Lukas Nmecha's debut and, at the end of the game, as he walked off, she asked for his shirt and he threw it to her! She was buzzing. 'Will I get a players shirt every time, Dad?' she asked.

He didn't really turn out to be a great loan signing for us but his kind gesture ignited the spark and, although she may never get a player's shirt again, my Daughter has definitely got the PNE bug.

All my mates are North End fans and there's no better feeling than a Preston goal.

I remember Scarborough away in 1996. When Gary Bennet scored the winning goal, he jumped into the away end right where I was standing. And then that Mark Rankine goal against Birmingham in the play-offs. It felt like the roof blew off!

Supporting PNE is everything.

All of my family holidays have been made short so we're back for the start of the season and there are no weekends away when it's a North End game. I love the fact that within 45 minutes of Preston there's all these so-called big clubs and yet non like ours, the original Invincibles.

JOHN GARRATT

At the end of Alan Jones' stint as Chairman, the club was in very dire financial straits and one of the directors, Barney Campbell, came round saying, 'Look, the club is going out of business tomorrow unless we find a quarter of a million pounds.'

Twenty of us were to put £12,500 each into the club. We were promised that if you put your money in, you could become a director and we all wanted to be a director of North End didn't we, so I joined up. Keith Leeming was appointed Chairman and me and Malcolm Woodhouse the Vice Chairmen. That was in 1982 and I was a director until 1996.

How Garratt's came to be shirt sponsors actually started with a dinner at the Grosvenor Hotel in London. Garratt's were Lloyd's Insurance Brokers at the time and I'd arranged the annual Lloyd's Brokers Dinner at the Grosvenor. Sitting next to me that evening was a chap I'd known as a young insurance salesman who'd recently been appointed the MD of Lombard Elizabethan. As the night wore on and the drink went down, I said to him, 'Look, you're the Managing Director of a relatively small insurance company, could you do with the national exposure of a Football League club by virtue of sponsoring their shirts and other things?'

He said, 'Well, what would it cost?' At the time, the club's only sponsor was its first sponsor, Trevor Hemmings' Pontins, so I made a figure up and said it would be something like £25,000 a year for three years which was five times what we were then getting. I then got hold of the menu card – I can't find the damn thing now – and I wrote on it '£25,000 a year for three years. Sign here:' and he wrote back, 'Subject to Garratt's Insurance Brokers giving us £1m of business per year.' So it became a business relationship.

Now, we were not doing well. We got relegated and then had to apply for re-election and Lombard, having merged to become Lombard Continental, withdrew from the sponsorship at the end of their second year. I felt very responsible as I had brought them to the club and here they were reneging on the deal. I decided, as the boss of Garratt's at the time, that we had to take it up so the sponsor changed from Lombard Continental to Garratt's Insurance and that's how it all came about, with a very huge dinner in the Grosvenor and something written on the back of a menu card.

Fortunately, our sponsorship coincided with the turning point of John McGrath's appointment. John was a real character. He turned up once at a board meeting and said, 'Mr Chairman, I want Frank Worthington' and Keith Leeming, as ever, said, 'We can't bloody afford Frank Worthington!'

'Ah yes, Mr Chairman, but he will put £2,000 on the gate every time he plays so we can afford him.' John could be tough but he also brought fun back to the club with his irrepressible humour and, oh, the players we had then – Gary Brazil, John Thomas, Bob Atkins – that was my favourite time of watching North End.

'Preston means a huge amount to me and PNE is absolutely a big part of that.'

I was privileged to be a fan during the whole of Sir Tom Finney's career having first gone on in 1937 when I was aged five. I was like everybody. Once you are a North Ender, you are a North Ender.

Photo (L to R) Richard Garratt, John Garratt.

JOHN SWINDELLS

I think it was in the spring of the 1956/57 season when my Dad first took me on for a night match against Burnley. To walk up the tunnel and actually see a floodlit ground at the age of six or seven, it was like, wow!

I remember having to push through to the cinder track carrying one of these little stools. Dad would take me down to the front and then meet me after the game. My Grandmother lived on Skeffington Road so we'd normally walk down there to her house for tea and then go home.

Dad's family ran a Post Office in Manchester. During the war he'd been away on convoy duty for quite some time and when he returned, the whole street had been bombed and flattened. His family were all okay but they were relocated from Manchester to a Post Office in New Longton so that's how he came to be in Preston.

Dad was a mad keen United fan and so we started alternating between Old Trafford and Deepdale, but we ended up as a family of six so money must've got a bit scarce and he finally said, 'Look, you've got to make your mind up. I can't afford to take you every week so who do you want to support?'

'By then I was hooked on North End and there was no question. No, it was never a question.'

Hopefully that was the only time I disappointed him.

I remember meeting Alex Dawson. I think every boy of my age, if you were a North Ender, wanted to be Alex Dawson. I've not seen a centre-forward near as good. He was a big bustling striker and players used to bounce off him.

He was only small but was one of the best headers of the ball.

I was lucky to be Mayor of Preston when it was Sir Tom's 90th and we had a celebration dinner at the Guild Hall. Well, Alex Dawson was there that night and I spent quite a bit of time with him. We were at the same table and I swapped places with my Daughter so I could sit next to him.

Sometimes you're told that you shouldn't meet your heroes but I had one of the best nights listening to his tales. I think he was probably the best buy North End ever made. £20,000 I think it was. They really should have gone up in the 1963/64 season. Don Revie's Leeds went up that year and we absolutely battered them 2-0 at Deepdale. It's possibly the finest performance I've ever seen from North End, and that Leeds team had the likes of Johnny Giles, Billy Bremner and Norman Hunter – all the players that went on to dominate British football.

In 1985, I was part of North End's lowest ever home crowd. I walked to Clifton Village from BNFL to watch them play Scunthorpe. We had to play in the afternoon instead of the evening as the floodlights were deemed unsafe.

I took half a day off work and three or four of us walked down from Springfields to Clifton Village and then got the bus to Moor Park. I can't quite remember the date but at the time the club was in big trouble and we lost 1-0. I also made the trip to Torquay that season for the match between the two bottom clubs.

Supporting North End has given me some of the highest highs and some of the lowest lows, but it's great to be part of the Preston family, and that really is what it is, a family.

JONNY NELSON

My earliest memories of going on North End were in the John Beck days. I was about four or five when my Dad, who also served as Club Chaplain, started dragging me along with my older Brother and Sister.

I absolutely hated it; hauled away from Saturday cartoons to sit in the freezing cold watching a ball lumped down a plastic pitch. He'd often find me with my coat zipped up over my head like a cocoon and he'd threaten never to take me again.

We were living in Blackburn at the time and supporting a side that was languishing in the old Third Division as all my mates were living the dream at the top of Premier League. It was a tough pill to swallow.

Thankfully for me, adolescence coincided with a turnaround in the club's fortunes, first under Gary Peters then David Moyes and later, Billy Davies. As I grew to better understand and love the game, we were treated to promotions, play-off campaigns and an arguably more cultured, entertaining style of football. The years of '96 to '06 were basically a ten-year honey trap, leaving me emotionally shackled for life.

'The most thrilling game I ever watched was the Birmingham play-off home leg in 2001.'

There was so much drama. My nerves were already shot by the time Mark Rankine popped up in the 92nd minute to take us into extra time. I remember calling my mum on my BT Cellnet mobile brick when Trevor Francis tried to lead his team off the field in protest but my voice had completely gone. It was before all the cynicism kicked in from so many near-misses and disappointments. We were small, but we had belief. It was like destiny was on our side. That was probably the most naive I've ever been, but it was nice.

I feel like I've ranted about North End pretty much everywhere I've worked to anyone who'd listen, often to people who'd rather not. From old colleagues at the Premier League like Phil Neville, Kevin Kilbane, Peter Drury and Jon Champion, to bemused American film stars like Samuel L. Jackson and Will Ferrell. I even had a great chat with Maradona's barber in Buenos Aires during the filming of The Football Show for Sky. I left him a classic Pontins shirt as a keepsake.

However, by far, my favourite conversation has been with actor, Bill Nighy. Early in our interview he asked me where I was from and then, without even the mention of football, regaled me with PNE facts and former players. He even remembered we'd had Beckham on loan. I think we spoke about his latest film at some stage but ended on the topic of a DVD he'd been watching about free kicks.

There have been so many players I've enjoyed watching over the years, albeit not always the biggest names on the team sheet. There are players I've loved to watch with the ball and those I've admired for their dependability, passion and aggression, but if I had to choose one it'd be 'Super' Jonny Macken. He knew how to mix it up and where the net was. For a couple of years he was unstoppable. And we had the same name, which helped.

One year, I was stood in the Sir Tom Finney family stand during an end of season celebration when I realised the man himself was stood just a few yards away from me. He kindly agreed to sign my scarf and I've treasured it ever since. Sadly, in the spirit of getting the most of your Sunday best, I've continued to wear the scarf for years, leaving it in dire need of a clean.

Photo courtesy of Jonny Nelson.

KARA LEE

M

y first memory as a Preston North End supporter is when I was part of the half-time penalty shootout with my football team of that time, Myerscough under eight Whites.

My Dad had let me get a PNE shirt beforehand as I'd played in a game earlier and got hit in the face with the ball and was very upset. Dad would never let me have a PNE shirt before then as he supports Aston Villa, but I will come to that later. We were playing against QPR that day and I got to watch the game with some of my teammates. At half-time, we went onto the pitch and I was so excited. When it came to my penalty, I scored. I was so happy!

I have two favourite players. Number one is Paul Gallagher. I look up to him and want to be as good as him, if not better. I also have a framed away shirt with a message to me from Paul Gallagher written on it. My second favourite is Jayden Stockley, and I have a funny story about him. I was at my friend's one day playing out and she said a PNE player lives a few doors away. I wanted to go and see as I didn't really believe her so I went round to the house and Jayden answered the door. I said, 'Alright?' and my friend said, 'See, I told you!' and we ran back to her house.

Later that day we decided to post him a note as I wanted his autograph. I wrote 'Please can you sign my ball?' and put my name and address on it. A few days later Jayden came round to my house with a sharpie to sign my ball. I was so shocked and happy. He was lovely and chatted to me about my football playing whilst my Mum found the ball I wanted signing. He then signed the ball and went home.

My favourite game is PNE v Aston Villa on the 1st October 2016. As a treat for my Brother – who also supports Aston Villa like my Dad – we all went and sat in the away end. I had an Aston Villa shirt on but, inside, I was secretly up for PNE as my Dad wouldn't let me support them. Well, the game ended 2-1 to PNE. Yes! Not long after that match, my Dad finally decided to give up trying to turn me into a

Villa fan and let me support my hometown team. My Mum now takes me on Deepdale every month, if I'm good.

'For my 10th birthday my Grandad paid for me to be a mascot at the PNE v West Brom game on the 2nd December 2019.'

Sadly, we lost 1-0 as they scored a penalty in the final minutes but the evening was great. I got a tour of the stadium, went in the dressing rooms and met nearly all the players. The ones I didn't see, I saw after the game as we waited outside for them. And I got to walk out on the pitch with Jayden Stockley. I asked him for one of his shirts afterwards and he gave me one with a message on it. It was the best PNE experience and even losing didn't make me disappointed.

Supporting PNE is great. I love football and all my school friends follow PNE so we chat about them at breaks and lunchtimes. I sometimes go on PNE with my friend too, so that makes it fun!

4
TEAMS

ADRIAN WARD

PNE CRICKET CLUB

helped Ben Rhodes re-establish the cricket arm of the club after I joined North End's media and marketing department in 2007.

Ben's dream of bringing the team back to life was helped considerably by having a new colleague with a shared desire to play cricket and, alongside making up the numbers on the field, I held the role of Cricket Secretary until 2018 and set up our website and social media channels. We have a nucleus of around twenty players made up of employees of the football club, friends and some very passionate supporters. We play our home games at Riverside and compete in the Coupe Bradbury Solicitors Cricket League which primarily takes place in the villages north of Preston on Wednesday evenings in a 20/20 format.

Graeme Atkinson and Andy Fensome have been regulars since the team was re-established and a few of the current first team squad are keen to play when they can. Jayden Stockley even set up his own track at home during lockdown to practice his bowling! He netted alongside Tom Barkhuizen, Billy Bodin, Ryan Ledson and Ben Pearson during the off season so we hope they'll play a few games when circumstances allow.

Andy Lonergan made a quiet cameo appearance for us in 2019, a throwback to a decade earlier when he appeared in friendlies alongside Neil Mellor, Chris Neal and Sean St Ledger. Chris Neal had played U17 cricket for Hertfordshire and was a cut above with the best fielding arm I've ever seen in a club fixture! We've also had Ian Bryson, Scott Laird and Steve Wilkes turn out for us while Jack Cudworth often kept wicket when he was goalkeeper in the reserves and youth team.

In 2009, amidst rumours he was all set for a big money move to Middlesbrough, Sean St Ledger gave us all a heart-in-the-mouth moment when he got injured in a game at Chorley St James. Fielding in the deep, he somehow managed to stand on the ball and rolled his ankle. As he hobbled off, we all looked at each other, fearing the wrath of Derek Shaw and Alan Irvine for potentially costing the club millions! Luckily, Sean managed to walk it off and passed the medical but he then ended the deal of his own accord when he aborted the initial loan deal a few months later!

Our history is a very important to us and whenever something of significance involving the Lilywhites' cricket heritage is uncovered, it's quickly shared amongst our WhatsApp group. It's amazing to see the calibre of player that took cricket just as seriously as their fooball during their time at North End, especially in the 50s and 60s. We also wanted to acknowledge our heritage when creating our badge so we adapted the first official version of the Football Club's crest and also added a star above the shield in recognition of our one trophy win so far: the 2017 Boddington's League Cup!

Virtually every time we welcome a debutant, they go home saying, 'I'm going to tell everyone I've played for North End!' The fact that it's cricket rather than football doesn't take away any sense of pride. Most people that play for us get the chance to take the field alongside names they've cheered from the terraces so it makes it a very special team to represent. You can see what it means to the former players too.

PNE is a club that captures the heart of those who represent it and we all feel a sense of duty to keep this team thriving, to be good ambassadors for a famous sporting institution and uphold its great reputation.

Facebook: www.facebook.com/PNECC
Twitter: @PNE_CC

Photo (Top R): Adrian and Rowan Ward.
Photos courtesy of Adrian Ward and PNECC.

MURIEL FREEMAN
PRESTON NORTH END WOMEN'S JUNIOR FC

am the Secretary and Treasurer to Preston North End Women's Junior Football Club, having joined the club in 2001 as Treasurer.

We are a friendly, welcoming club with a strong competitive spirit, and are one of the few girls' football clubs in the North West of England that have teams at every age level from a U9 development squad (for school years 4 and 5) through to U16.

We are now in the process of coming under the umbrella of PNE Community and Education Trust, and the revival of the PNE Women's team and PNEW Development Squad ensures that our junior players have a pathway into senior football. Our players, other than our U9s, U10s and U11s, play in competitive league and cup competitions and all our teams participate in a number of tournaments every season to enhance the playing experience.

Players join us from all over the North West, going as far north as Barrow-in-Furness and as far south as Manchester and Cheshire. Our Managers and Coaches all hold FA coaching qualifications and are FA DBS cleared. All our goalkeepers receive specialist training as well as training with their teams on a Thursday evening. Our home games are played at UCLan Sports Arena in Preston, one of the best facilities in the county, and all our training sessions also take place at the £12m complex.

Our ethos is to develop each of our players and teams to be the best they can be in a safe and competitive, but enjoyable, environment. And we are proud to say that a number of our players have achieved county and international recognition.

During the years, I've been fortunate to meet some good people who have spent years giving their time and commitment in various roles. Not to mention the parents who fully support their girls, taking them to training and games week in and week out.

It's very difficult to pick one favourite memory throughout my time with the Club – there's been so many! I have seen our teams win many cup finals and league trophies and the joy the girls show in their achievements is always a special moment. In more recent years, going back to 2016, our U16s went to Dallas, Texas, USA, to compete in the renowned Dallas Tournament. Girls from our club then went on to achieve college scholarships in the USA as a direct result of taking part in that tournament. This fantastic end of season experience has now been available to our U16s ever since, and in 2019, our then U16s chose to visit Denmark to compete in the prestigious Dana Cup against teams from all over the world.

In 2018/19, our U14s had an outstanding all-conquering season winning every competition they entered! In the West Lancs Girls U14s League they didn't lose a game. They won the West Lancs Girls U14s League Cup, the Lancs FA U14s County Cup and then, to cap it all, won the ESF National Tournament Trophy. For this, they went to Skegness at Easter and won the Regional Tournament which lead to them going to St George's Park in July for the Nationals which they won!

My aim in volunteering with the club has always been to provide the opportunity for girls to play football for their enjoyment. We run an open training session each June giving girls an opportunity to see whether they are interested in joining our club, and people can get involved by making contact with either myself, our club Chairman, Mark Roskell, or any of our individual managers or coaches.

www.pnewjfc.com
Twitter: @PNEWJFC

Photo credits: Muriel Freeeman and PNEWJFC.
Team photo: PNEWJFC U14s, 2018-19.

JIMMY ATKINSON

PNE SUPPORTERS TEAM, MANAGER

W e've been a part of the IFA – the Internet Football Association – since 2015, but there's been a supporters team throughout the years. In fact, John Lee, who was part of the old ISA, managed a team in the mid-90s which Gary Peters played for!

In the IFA, we've won the League eight times and the Cup five times. The IFA is great because it brings supporters together through football. It's not every day you play ninety minutes of football before going to support your team for another ninety!

I remember when we played Ipswich away on a bank holiday Saturday in August. It was a 12:30pm kick-off moved for Sky. PNE won 4-0. Nugent scored and bowed before their fans which wound them up no end! We had a game ourselves against Ipswich Supporters that morning at 9am so Steve Cowell, who used to manage the team, took us down in a minibus at three in the morning. I think we won 8-3, and then to see PNE win in the afternoon was amazing.

We are open to any player who is a PNE fan, no matter of standard. The majority of us are season ticket holders and some of us used to sit together on the Kop back in the day.

'We've grown up together, been to each other's weddings and had holidays together. There's a real family feeling.'

We've had great support from the club and have played on Deepdale a few times. Derek Shaw was very good, and obviously Steve Cowell is now the Kit Man so any kit and training tops come to us instead of going in a skip! Also, we have the Ghanian PNE Supporters, and Ted Phibson – Tetley Ted –

goes out twice a year to Ghana and takes kit from the club and anything we can give too. His commitment to them is amazing!

Steve is very busy now but comes and supports us when he can. Derek Shaw would come and watch us, Matt Jackson, the physio, has played a couple of times. There's a picture somewhere of Neil Mellor and Barry Nicholson watching us at MK Dons and Bailey Wright once even played for us. Bailey came over when he was sixteen and, whilst he was waiting for his work permit, he came down and played for us against Halifax. You could tell he had something about him. He scored a goal and then after the match Steve Cowell bundled him into the back of his drinks van, sat him on some crates and drove him back home!

One year, we played Stockport County at home in the quarter-final of the Cup and Billy Davies was watching as there was some bounce game going on. Anyway, we were getting changed and he pops in! We were a bit awestruck at the time because PNE were on the verge of the play-offs and he was revolutionising the club.

I'll never forget the team talk he gave us. It really got you going. Stockport were top of the league but we went 8-0 up and I put a lot of it down to his team talk. He made you feel ten feet tall! You could really see how he got the best out of his team at the time. He literally made you feel invincible. You could tell why PNE went 22 games unbeaten that season, because he made you feel like you could do anything. The game actually finished 8-3 as I went in nets for the last fifteen minutes and conceded three. That's another reason why I'll never forget it!

ALISTAIR WHITE
PNE WALKING FOOTBALLERS

The best thing about being involved with walking football is seeing so many people turn up wanting to take part in a sport they have loved their whole lives. It's great to see their passion and determination to play the beautiful game each week.

Despite some facing injuries or some not being as able as others, nobody ever gives up. What's even better is that the games are always played in the right manner and attitude. There's a real community feel. Everyone is together.

Aimed at the over 50s, walking football is designed to help people keep an active lifestyle despite their age, as well as getting those back playing football who have had to stop due to injuries. It's non-contact and anyone who jogs or sprints while the ball is in play will be penalised with a free kick awarded to the other team. It's a welcoming environment and there is never any conflict between players. It's a place for anyone over the age of fifty, male or female, no matter your ability or mobility. It is all about being active, having fun together and playing the game you love.

We have many different teams and we enter various walking football competitions if players wish to be considered for them. For the players to be able to pull on a PNE shirt, to represent PNECET and really feel part of the club, I think it's a massive opportunity for them. To have that chance to wear the shirt, a club some have supported their whole lives, is huge. We're very proud of our players and their achievements. We've even had some players selected for England which is amazing!

We now have 118 walking footballers across all sessions and, in normal circumstances, run three sessions per week. The first is on Tuesdays from 6:30pm until 7:30pm. On Thursdays, from 6:30pm to 7:30pm, we run a women's only session (for any age), and our last and most popular session is every Friday, 11am until 1pm. The first hour on Fridays is walking football and the following hour is a social hour. This allows all participants to enjoy refreshments whilst socialising with one another which usually turns into them complaining about the staff's refereeing decisions!

I first started working on the programme back in March 2018 as a volunteer as part of my university work. I was asked to ref a game at my first session. I hadn't done much walking football before but, to their credit, the players recognised this and were so good with me. Then in September 2019 (after graduating from uni) I got a full-time role at Preston North End Community and Education Trust and I now work at the sessions every week.

We have a great team on the programme and we're very lucky to have Melissa Brown, Hannah White, James Stansfield and Rob Walker as coaches. We don't really do structured coaching. The sessions are more about being inclusive and helping people get and stay active. We comment on nice play but we don't try and coach anyone to play a certain way, even at the tournaments. We just help with the organisation and point out a few things, and besides, most of our players have many more years' experience of walking football than I have!

All our sessions take part at the PNE Community Training Centre, PlayFootball, PR2 3TX. To get involved you can email me or any of our walking football coaches, or you can just turn up fifteen minutes before the session starts. Everyone is welcoming and encouraging which creates a real positive atmosphere, so no one should ever be nervous about joining or taking part!

Email: alistair.white@pne.com

Photo credits (Clockwise L to R): Ian Robinson, John Wilson, Bev Taylor.

1875

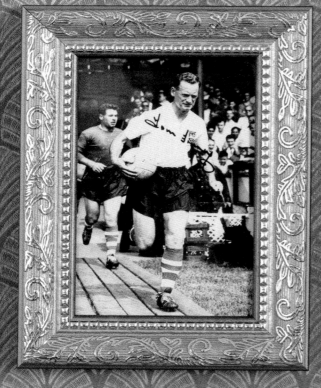

GREAT RELA-TIONS

ALAN KELLY JUNIOR

ALAN KELLY SNR – FATHER

In 1971, when PNE were at home to Oxford, my Dad was carried off after getting smashed with thirty mins to go. PNE were down to ten men but Dad was a good outfield player and, with his arm in a sling, went back on to play on the left wing.

PNE won 1-0 and Dad said he nearly set up a second when he nutmegged Ron Atkinson!

I used to be taken along to training at PNE every day during the school holidays and to every home game too, so growing up, it felt like it was the normal thing to do. Obviously, football was a world away from what it is today with the 24/7 media cycle, and Mum and Dad never made a big deal of Dad's status at PNE or with the Republic of Ireland. It was only later that I could reflect on what he had achieved in football.

I remember Dad's testimonial match in 1973 after a bad shoulder injury had ended his playing career. I was only five and it was my first match at PNE. We took our seats in the West Stand on the old wooden benches, but along with the 5,000+ PNE fans, we couldn't see the pitch as a thick fog had descended on Deepdale. We couldn't see a thing, but they still played the full ninety minutes!

Fans of a certain age will remember that the great Brian Clough used to have his son, Nigel sat next to him in the dugout at Nottingham Forest and Dad did the same with me at PNE! There would be Manager, Nobby Stiles, my Dad the Assistant Manager, the sponge man, 2 subs and me sat at in the home team dugout.

'I witnessed all the emotion of the game from the coaching team's viewpoint.'

The fans reactions, the ebb and flow of the match and the final result. I also got to dive into the giant bath afterwards which was the size of a small swimming pool. Funnily, Dad always had a cigarette in his hand in the dugout but never smoked. He would go through a packet a game and the old kit man, who did smoke, used to wait with glee to collect them at the end!

The day after a home match, Dad would take us back to Deepdale and, while he was busy with his coaching work, we'd be allowed on the pitch to have a game of football.

Dad would come out and take a few pot shots at us in the goals and groundsman, Peter McCallion would join in and we'd recreate the action from Saturday's match. Who would've thought that ten years later I'd be following in my Dad's footsteps as a goalkeeper at PNE? I think he was very proud when I made my debut because he never expected it to happen. I was an apprentice electrician at sixteen and I don't think Dad ever thought I'd be a pro-footballer by the age of seventeen!

I was born into and brought up with PNE. I played and coached for the club for over 400 games, and winning promotion in 2015 via the Play-Off Final at Wembley seemed to complete the circle started by Dad's FA Cup Final Wembley appearance in 1964. I think I'm right in saying that our combined years at PNE went unbroken from 1958-1992 – 34 years in total. Preston North End meant everything to Dad, and when they named the Town End after him, he and all of us were immensely proud.

Photo (courtesy of Alan Kelly Jr): Alan Kelly Jr., Bertie Kelly.

BRIAN FINNEY

SIR TOM FINNEY – FATHER

As a child, I was always aware that there was something different about my Dad due to the number of times people would stop us to request an autograph or have a photograph with him, usually to Mother's annoyance!

Dad had lots of stories and probably the one he always told was set, I think, back in the late 1948/49 season when North End were playing Sunderland at Roker Park and Bill Shankly had been dropped to 12th man. On the way there, Bill was sat next to Dad on the coach, and obviously disappointed not to be playing forecast a defeat. However, we won and, on the way back, Bill said to Dad, 'That's the worst bloody Sunderland side he'd ever seen.'

My own experiences of following PNE came mainly after Dad had retired as I was away at boarding school and only got home for the odd Saturday game. But after my Son was born and he got interested, we hardly missed a game, home or away. As for my first time watching PNE, I can't remember exactly if it was my first game, but the 1954 FA Cup Final was certainly one of my earliest. What a disappointment for Dad, the team and all the supporters. He probably shouldn't have played due to injury, but there we go.

'Probably one of the most memorable matches I saw was Dad's final game in 1960, but there were so many other great matches and memories made.'

Obviously, his knighthood and becoming a Freeman of Preston stand out.

Dad did an awful lot for charities and I have taken over some of his work with Baby Beat, The Space Centre and The Alzheimer's Society.

I treasure my connection with the club and it's a privilege to be able to sit in the Director's Box and to see the fantastic Splash statue every time I visit for a home match.

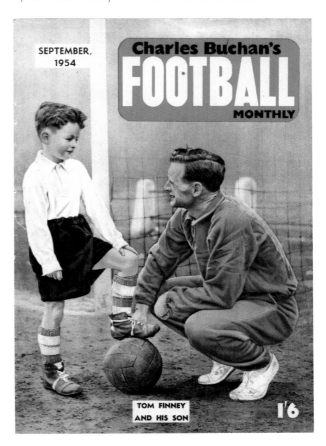

SEPTEMBER, 1954

Charles Buchan's FOOTBALL MONTHLY

TOM FINNEY AND HIS SON

1'6

CHRIS SHANKLY
BILL SHANKLY – GRANDFATHER

My Grandad signed for Preston North End from Carlisle as a wing-half in 1933 and had a great career at Deepdale but sadly, war arrived in 1939 just off the back of North End winning the FA Cup in '38.

He was 26 I think. At the peak of his playing career really. To come back then, after the war, in his early thirties near the end of his playing career, it's sad in some ways.

Whenever we take people around the hotel in Liverpool, we show the memorabilia we have on display and always point to his '38 FA Cup Winners and '37 Runners-up medals. I always say he probably would've had more medals if it hadn't been for the war. What could have been with that great side? We'll never know.

When we went to Preston with the new hotel, we reached out and connected to a lot of different people. We met with Peter Ridsdale at North End who was fantastic, and we got invited by the guys at the National Football Museum archives to have a look round. They showed us a few things including this huge book filled in by PNE staff back in the day. It was basically a record of players they were scouting and contained a few entries from when they'd gone to watch my Grandad playing for Carlisle, and pretty much most of them weren't great!

Comments read something like 'really enthusiastic, but a lot to learn about the game and the technical side', that sort of thing. They weren't exactly complimentary! It didn't half bring a smile to my face. You'd have thought going off that, they'd never have signed him but obviously they saw something somewhere, and he had this brilliant time at North End and got capped by Scotland too.

Through our new hotel in Preston, we'll be telling his PNE story and displaying his old Preston shirts, boots, socks, match tickets, programmes and his PNE medals. When my Grandad signed for North End he actually signed the contract on his way from Carlisle to Preston on a train in a first class rail carriage.

From there came the idea to name the restaurant The Carriage and to have the décor for the restaurant and the reception area styled on a 1930s first class rail carriage.

Another big thing about his time at the club was his relationship with Sir Tom Finney. It's well documented that he was coming to the end of his career as Tom was coming through, but even right through to his dying day, my Grandad was adamant Finney was the greatest player he ever saw. They remained great friends throughout their lives so it's an important connection to us, and we've met with Brian Finney and the family – a lovely family – and we've a baseline agreement that when we open we can display some of Sir Tom's memorabilia, and do a Finney exhibit as well. We are also one of the headline sponsors of the Sir Tom Finney Soccer Centre, something we were more than honoured to do.

'For us, the main idea with the project of the hotels is to keep Bill Shankly's legacy alive.'

To show what he was as a person as well as highlighting his football creer and what he achieved. Our family stories are all about what he could do above and beyond for people. All he wanted to do was make people happy.

Now we're opening in Preston and the reaction has been great and I think my Grandad would've liked that, because Preston meant an awful lot to him.

MARK NAYLOR
WILLIAM NAYLOR – GREAT GRANDFATHER

Back in the 1960s and 70s, I played football in the local leagues for a club named Ashton Celtic. Moor Park was our home ground and also where we'd train during the week.

On the Saturdays, when PNE had a home match, we'd finish our game, get changed as fast as we could and rush over the road to catch the last ten or so minutes of the match. The gates were opened to let people out if they wanted to leave early and it also allowed us to nip in to see the end of the match!

Little did I know at that time that one of my ancestors was also connected with Moor Park and also, in a big way, with Preston North End. In fact, many years before me, he'd made the exact same trip across the road from Moor Park to help establish PNE's home on a parcel of land on Deepdale Farm.

It was forty years or so later when I discovered my connection with PNE when I began researching my family history. Whilst scanning the local papers for a photo of my Grandfather, Sidney Naylor – who sadly died in World War 1 in 1918 – I came across an article in the Lancashire Daily Post dated the 30th January 1905 which gave details on the death of Sidney's Father, my Great Grandfather, William Naylor.

In the article, it stated William was one of a group of cricketers who moved from 'the marshes' – now the Strand Road area – to Moor Park to play their matches. It would be members of this group of cricketers who would go on to become founders of PNE and make Deepdale its home ground! I couldn't believe my luck to have found this information, and Lady Luck struck again a few days later when I read in The Evening Post that Dr David Hunt, the Curator of the South Ribble Museum and author of *The History of Preston North End Football Club* was to give a talk at the Museum on the origins of PNE. Of course I went, and I was thrilled to bits when David actually mentioned my Great Grandfather's name!

At the end of the talk, David asked for any questions. I put my hand up to explain and also to check if this William Naylor he had mentioned was my Great Grandfather and indeed he was!

Later on, we had a chat and David gave me a lot more information about William which he'd found out when writing his book on PNE. It was amazing to find that my Great Grandfather was one of the original founders of our club that started out playing cricket and rugby before turning to football. I also learned it was William, as Club Secretary, who posted the advert in 1875 promoting PNE's first ever game of cricket at their new Deepdale home. The rest, as they say, is history!

It's been fascinating going through the papers to discover more about my Great Grandfather's involvement with PNE, and to see how the club went from humble beginnings to the Invincibles of the football world. I hope my interview gives encouragement and hope to anyone researching their own ancestors as you just never know what you'll find! And if you find you have descendants with the surname of Naylor, Parkinson or Jackson, – William Naylor married Margaret Alice Parkinson and Sidney Naylor married Minnie Jackson – then you too may have a connection to the birth of PNE!

Annual TEA PARTY and CONCERT will be held on Easter Monday evening, in Bow-lane School.—Tickets 1s each.

PRESTON NORTH END CRICKET CLUB.—
Opening Game, Saturday, March 27th, on private ground at Deepdale.—WM. NAYLOR, Hon. Sec.

BLACKPOOL CONSERVATIVE ASSOCIATION.
A GRAND BANQUET, under the auspices of the

MICHAEL TURLEY
FRED DEWHURST – GREAT, GREAT UNCLE

We are five Brothers: Frank, David, Ged, Mark and me, and Fred Dewhurst is our Great-great-Uncle on our Mother's side.

Around 1995/96 I bought shares in North End and the shares certificate came with a picture of the Invincibles on it. I framed it for my Son, Luke to put on his bedroom wall as I wanted him to be a North End fan. When I showed it me Mum she said, 'Where's Uncle Freddie?' I said, 'What you on about?' She said, 'Uncle Freddie!' I didn't know what she was on about so I asked round a bit and that's how I found out about our connection to Fred Dewhurst.

'I'd lived 35 years without knowing. It was a total surprise.'

I mentioned it to my Brother, Frank who knew a little about it growing up. Our Grandad was a season ticket holder and a real die-hard North Ender, and Frank said he'd mentioned it but nothing great was made about it. So Frank was aware of it, but only as much as that we had a relative who used to play for North End. It wasn't the days of the internet where everything was at hand. Only later, when I mentioned it, did we really start to investigate and find out who Fred really was, and what a career he'd had!

We realised not just how good a player he'd been but also how important he was to the club. He played mostly as an inside left-forward and scored North End's first ever League goal, played for England nine times (scoring eleven goals), captained the Invincibles double-winning team of 1888-89, and was also the Club Secretary.

Frank remembers there used to be a blue and white Wedgewood cheese plate that was sort of a family heir-loom and referred to as a belonging to Fred. Apparently all the players had once been given gifts by Stoke when they played down there.

Fred was an amateur footballer – a rare thing amongst the professionals of the Invincibles – and earned his living as a teacher at Preston Catholic College. In fact, when they won the FA Cup in 1889, he brought it into to the school the following week to show all the kids.

On top of everything else, he helped out at the Unicorn Pub. He was based there because his brother had died and he was helping his sister-in-law with the kids and the running of the pub. When you put all these things together you wonder how on earth he found the time. He must've always been on the move!

When PNE opened the Invincibles stand, they invited people associated to different members of the Invincibles as guests of honour. It was a match against Burnley and before kick-off they'd placed a life-size cut out of each Invincible around the centre circle. We went along with two of our Cousins, but there's certainly more than just us in Preston who are related. There's the Dewhurst family, our Cousins, and there'll be others elsewhere no doubt – it's not just us!

As a player, it's said he could play any way along the front line. He was physical but talented and, while he made the most of his robust frame, he was also a fine dribbler and finisher. Fred was born and bred in Preston. His roots were here and he remained here until he died in 1895 at the very young age of 31. We're all very proud of our ties to Fred. As PNE fans alone, the Invincibles mean a lot to us. Supporting the club is in the family, in the blood, but the fact the connection is there adds something more, it's a nice feeling, absolutely.

Photo (L to R): Frank and Michael Turley.

TOM SMITH
TOM SMITH – FATHER

W
hen playing for North End, my Dad, Tom Smith, lived on St Thomas Road and shared with Bobbie Beattie. On match days, they would mingle with the fans walking to the ground and always enjoyed meeting and chatting with them.

Dad was a centre-back and played for Kilmarnock in Scotland where he was born. In 1936, he transferred to North End for a fee of £2,000. He played three times for Scotland and, when he finished playing for PNE in 1945, he went back to Kilmarnock to become their manager. When his managerial career finished he then moved back to live in Preston.

Dad was captain when PNE won the FA Cup in 1938. In those days, the players were presented with medals at the end of the match but then had to hand them back to get their names engraved on them. But being the captain, Dad had to rush off to the BBC studios to do an interview for a programme they called In Town Tonight It was what they called a 'light programme' and was on at 8pm. By the time he came back from the studios it was too late for him to hand his medal back so he was too late to get his name engraved on it. It might be unique as the only Cup-winning captain's medal without a name on it!

He was also captain for the War Cup victory over Arsenal in 1941. The first match at Wembley ended 1-1 and the replay was three or four weeks later at Blackburn Rovers. North End won 2-1 with two goals from Bobbie Beattie. You can see the game on Pathé News on YouTube. There are very few photographs of the game but, as it was wartime, there may have been certain restrictions.

Watching the game, you can see the differences to today. They do congratulate each other when a goal is scored but there's no bouncing and sliding on their knees. It's quite different, and diving after being fouled was not even thought about!

Dad told me about one match where this centre-forward – I can't remember who – was

a rough player and was dishing it out so Dad clattered him early on and the ref came up to him and said, 'I'll watch the centre-forward, you just watch the football.' And that was it. He said there was a lot more respect for the refs in those days.

I have Dad's medals which I treasure, and the actual ball from the 1938 Cup Final which is signed by all eleven players. Interestingly, Shankly signed it 'William Shankly'. I can't find it now, but there used to be a mark on the ball where George Mutch's penalty struck the crossbar as it went in. Dad knew where it was but I think it must've worn off over time. I've actually taken the ball along to a match at Deepdale to show some fans I know who sit near me. I was clutching it tightly all game and didn't dare put it down on the ground!

The funny thing is that when Mutch got fouled, there was a bit of a delay before he got to his feet and so there was doubt as to whether he would be able to take the penalty. Mutch was the designated taker so my Dad was relieved when George got to his feet because he'd made up his mind as captain that he should take it himself.

Through my Dad, I've always had this loyalty to PNE. There's never been a question about any other team. It's my club.

THE FOOTBALLER
OF THE YEAR
FOR THE SECOND TIME.

PRESENTED TO
TOM FINNEY.
PRESTON NORTH END F.C.
BY THE
FOOTBALL WRITERS ASSOCIATION.
MAY, 1957

PRIZED

POSSESSIONS

ANDREW DODWELL

I came to support Preston through my Grandparents, Margaret and Ken Chambers. My Nanna especially was a massive fan and used to stand on the old Kop end. She took me on at any opportunity and I've never looked back.

I went to Wembley in 1994 when I was eight years old. I remember my Dad driving us down to Watford and us taking the Underground to Wembley where we met the rest of the family. I also recall there being a lot more North End fans than Wycombe fans.

I was once a mascot against Wigan at Deepdale but a couple of days after, I got knocked over and the North End shirt I was given as a mascot was ruined from the incident. My Mother managed to get hold of Ian Bryson and explained what had happened and he kindly invited me to be mascot against Blackpool at Deepdale. I got another free kit, met the players again and also met Sir Tom Finney. It was a fantastic day! Then a few weeks later my parents received a call from North End asking if I wanted to be mascot for Burnley away.

We arrived at Turf Moor a little too early and I was sat in the changing rooms by myself when I was asked if I wanted to go onto the pitch and kick a ball around. I was on the pitch on my own in an empty Turf Moor for around twenty minutes. It was a little scary to be honest. When I returned to the changing rooms, I was asked if I'd like to be a ball boy for the game. It was a strange evening, but one I enjoyed!

I have a good collection of PNE shirts but wish I had more, especially the striped Coloroll away shirt. The first shirt I got was the white Baxi one from our Division Three promotion season. In total, I currently have 41 shirts. My favourite is a white Coloroll one. It was my Nanna's and is something I will always treasure.

Following PNE means everything to me, and I've played for the Supporters Team since 2005. It's been a fantastic journey. We've been very successful and I've made some great friends and memories along the way. We travel up and down the country playing football and getting to represent the club we love. I'm still trying to get up and down the pitch, even after all these years. I think I still have a few more years left in me and as long as the team are going then so will I!

PNE have been a massive part of my life and my family's for many years and I'm hoping to carry that on through my Daughter. I currently go on North End with my Dad, Dale Dodwell, my Aunty, Sharon Conlin, and my Uncle, Martin Chambers, and for the past twenty years I've had the tradition of going to the Deepdale Labour Club before every game.

North End have always been there when I've needed them. When times were hard I knew that watching my team would help with any stress or upset I may have been feeling at that time. Yes, it's a rollercoaster ride being a Preston fan, but it's a fantastic club to follow. Seeing the same faces every week, either home or away, it's a proper family club and I would love nothing more than to see us in the Premier League, even if it's just for the one season!

DENNIS HIGGINS
1963 PHOTOGRAPHS

It was 1958 and I'll always remember it. We were playing Bolton and went on the West Stand Paddock. Dad put me through the juveniles turnstile and he went through the adults one. When I got through, there was a wall between us. I panicked. *Where's me dad?*

But thankfully we met up. There was no segregation and I was stood next to a woman who was a Bolton fan. In one hand, she swung a big heavy rattle which was hurting my ears and in the other held an actual pig's trotter! Afterwards I asked Dad why she had the trotter and he found out from work that Bolton were called The Trotters. She must've taken it to every game. That was my introduction to Deepdale – a pig's trotter!

On the 11th May 1963, I took a coach up north with mates, Ken Addison and John Mason, to watch North End play Newcastle United. It was a dead rubber with nothing at stake for either team, but stands out because Howard Kendall made his debut. I think it was Nobby Lawton who was injured, and Kendall was only sixteen or seventeen at the time. When I was going, my Mum suggested I take her old Brownie Box camera and get some photos and I'm glad I did.

We set off from Starch House Square in a Scout coach which was by no means full. We arrived early so took a walk around the ground. St James' Park looked very different in those days; the area was quite austere and grey. We didn't know where to go and just walked through a turnstile, ending up behind the goals opposite the Gallowgate end amongst all these Newcastle fans. I met up with Ken a few weeks ago and he said, 'Do you remember those Newcastle fans? They were throwing peanuts at us!' I said, 'Yeah, fancy that!' He said, 'well, better than 'em punching us in the face!'

They obviously knew we were PNE fans! The match ended 2-2. Dawson scored two and Kendall made his mark. That was virtually the Cup Final team of a year later. In all, it was a great day out in the north east. I kept the photos and programme for posterity and they're

significant, not just for Howard Kendall's debut, but also because John McGrath – our future manager – was playing centre-half for Newcastle!

I used to play for North End's Juniors and trained at Deepdale on Tuesday and Thursday nights. I'd rush home from school, have a bit of tea and walk it from Brookfield. You'd get nervous walking through the corridors at Deepdale then, thinking *this is where all the players are.*

There was a big kit box in the middle of the dressing room and one night we were all getting changed when Tom Finney walked in. 'Hello lads, can I get my kit out?' We were gobsmacked! He wore the same kit as us, those old baggy silk shorts and big white shirts – all too big for me! He wanted to keep fit for testimonial games and so joined in with us. We trained on that horrible pitch at the side of the ground. It was just muck with big chunky wooden goalposts. Lew Bradford and Walter Crook took training and really put us through our paces. You'd be running then all of a sudden you'd think I'm next to Tom Finney. Ha! He was such a gentleman. Even if you tackled him he'd say, 'Good tackle, son, keep that up.' You look back now and say crikey, I wish I'd made more of that!

DOUG SALLIS
BOB BOND PRINTS

My Dad loved football all his life but, bizarrely, never really supported a team. He worked for various breweries and moved around a lot so wherever he lived he'd follow the local team.

He worked in Great Yarmouth where I was born, and watched Norwich City. Then we moved to Bedford and he watched Luton Town. We moved to Preston when I was ten and, by then, I was already football mad. Dad would watch PNE one week and Blackburn the next. He wanted to get my Brother and I involved so one Saturday we went to watch Blackburn v Crystal Palace and the following Tuesday saw PNE v Gillingham. It was October 1987 and Oshor Williams scored in a 1-1 draw. Ever since – some 32 years later – I've been hooked on PNE and my Brother, sadly, hooked on Rovers. For the record, Dad retired and moved to Stevenage and, you've guessed it, followed Stevenage!

Around 1990, I was in the Junior Whites – 90p entry to games – and for home games a few of us were selected to take penalties at half-time. My turn was against Birmingham City on a dark Tuesday night on the plastic pitch. The younger kids went to the Kop end but as I was about thirteen. We were sent to take our kicks in front of approximately 3,000 Birmingham fans stood on the old Town End. We had three pens each.

My first strike sailed over the bar and up into the Birmingham fans. The Brummies wouldn't give the ball back, and then ditto for my second kick. Then one of the fellas running the shootout said to me, 'Bloody hell, Doug, we've only got one ball left. You better not put it into those fans again!'

Up I stepped for my third penalty. All Birmingham's fans giving it the 'WOOOOOOOOAH' noise as I ran up to the ball.I was so nervous, but I hit it sweetly . . . and scored! Everyone was relieved, none more so than me, but I honestly don't know if the Junior Whites ever got their balls back!

'That memory may be the reason I cheered so wildly when Mark Rankine scored in the Birmingham Play-off Semi in 2001.'

I cheered so loud I gave myself a migraine and literally saw stars and I blame Mark Rankine for the fact I've suffered from migraines ever since!

For my 23rd birthday I received a Bob Bond team print of the 1999/2000 Division Two champions. I loved it, and as I had no real commitments back then, I went and ordered Bob's whole collection – 75 PNE players on A5 cards at a cost of approximately £100. Over the years I've met various players and been lucky to get some of the cards signed, including Graham Alexander, David Eyres, Sir Tom, Alan Kelly, George Ross, John Thomas, Tommy Thompson and David Nugent. I'm a car salesman and have sold cars to Tony Ellis, David Moyes and Lee Ashcroft, but didn't get their cards signed – missed opportunities! But my favourite one is the one my Wife kindly got Bob to do of me for my 40th entitled 'Doug Sallis, PNE legend.' It takes pride of place in my hallway.

Only my Wife and Daughter mean more to me than PNE. I've been to countless games, home and away, and must've spent thousands on memorabilia, tickets, shirts etc. I even have a tattoo of the club crest on my right arm. I'd absolutely love us to get to the Premier League but, whatever happens, I'll support the boys until the day I die.

EDDIE MAYOR
PROGRAMME COLLECTOR

A friendly away at Workington in 1977 doesn't seem to be a highlight for any other North End fans, but it was for me.

Me and my best friend, Tom Coyne, had got there early doors for a 7pm kick-off and, although the pubs in Workington closed their doors at two, we ended up finding an all-day drinking bar at the Rugby club. After more than a few scoops, we arrived at the ground just as the team bus was pulling in. Next thing we knew, Harry Catterick pulled us on the bus, made a speech to the players about how they should be proud we'd turned up and then made every player shake our hands and thank us!

I got into football whilst at primary school. It wasn't North End or any club in particular, it was just football, any football. I watched North End, Blackburn and Leyland Motors whenever I could. Dad preferred cricket and was never big on football but my late Aunty Kath lived and breathed PNE. She knew I was watching North End regularly and couldn't believe it when I appeared on Match of the Day at Ewood Park when PNE were away. So after talking to my Uncle Eddie – another North Ender – they had a word in my ear and told me it was a family tradition to support PNE. I'm glad they did as I've never regretted it.

'I've passed the tradition on to my boys and fortunately they are now passing it on to their own.'

The first programme I ever got was PNE v Hull City 19th October 1968. I found it in the street near home and I still have it. I used to collect anything that resembled a programme. If it was a World Cup Final or Chorley v Gainsborough, I bought it!

I now have close to 2,000 home and around 1,300 away game programmes, but the one I probably pride above any other is one for the PNE v Liverpool friendly of 4th August, 1970. A rare item.

It was a night game I went to but, for some reason, having got the programme I either lost it, swapped it or just threw it away. I looked for a copy for nearly forty years to no avail. I checked every auction list going in the days before eBay and once bid up to £100 but never got a sniff. Then one day I saw it priced for £1 on a car boot and ended up paying just 50p!

One that continues to elude me is for a home game v Leeds on the 9th April 1962. I would love to have it because, if I got that, I'd have every home league game since the beginning of the 1959-60 season.

I've now started documenting my collection, listing the date of the game, the opponents, the result and the articles inside. I feel the programmes do need documenting in some way as I think the form is living on borrowed time with all the instant media we have now. At this early stage, it's for my own reference but I'm hoping, when it's complete, I can show it to other collectors and get their opinions. It's all about sharing information with fellow fans.

Supporting North End means the world to me. My friend, Tom, who I went to Workington with, sadly left us four years ago. He was the biggest PNE supporter ever and when he passed, our club placed his name on the fixture board outside Deepdale. Every Gentry Day, we remember the likes of Tom. That's what our club is to me, a brotherhood of friends.

Photo courtesy of Eddie Mayor.

EVIE BANKS
MATCH WORN SHIRT

The best match I've been to was the Play-off Final at Wembley in 2015. It was a great atmosphere and even better that we won. All the PNE fans were so happy and my Dad even cried!

My Dad has always supported PNE and he got me and my Brother into it. My first ever match was at Deepdale against Colchester in League One when I was just six years old. My Brother was a mascot that day and we got to meet Simon Grayson and all the players in the dressing room before the match. They were all really nice and I had my photo taken with Joey Garner. Since then, I've always supported Preston!

Seáni Maguire is one of my favourite players. Once, I was a mascot with the boys team I play for – Gregson Lane FC – when PNE played a friendly against Bamber Bridge. I really wanted to walk out with Seáni but sadly he wasn't there. During the match, my Dad managed to get the whole of the PNE squad to sign my green PNE top which has Maguire on the back, so everyone had signed it bar Seáni.

Then, on a league game at Deepdale, my Dad took a photo of me waiting near the player's tunnel at half-time. I was waiting for Seáni to spot me when the team came out for the second half, hoping he'd be able to sign my shirt, but he didn't see me. That night, my Dad tweeted the photo of me and tagged Seáni in it, saying his autograph was the only one missing. Sometime later, Seáni direct messaged my Dad saying he'd not only sign my green shirt but, at the next home game versus Bristol City, he would give me his match shirt and sign that for me too. I was so excited!

Arrangements were made for us all to meet after the game near the tunnel and Seáni even messaged my Dad on the day to double check we'd be there. When the match finished, I went to the bottom of the AKTE stand near the tunnel and I could see Seáni was looking for me. There were lots of other children there too who were all shouting for his shirt, but he came straight over and gave it to me. It was really busy and he couldn't sign it or take a photo so

later Seáni again messaged my Dad to say he would try and sign it at the next home game. It was a match against Barnsley and this time we went to the players' entrance, getting there early at 12:45.

'I had my photo taken with lots of PNE players and they were really nice, and Seáni finally signed my shirt!. He chatted with us and I was so excited I could hardly speak.'

I thanked him for all that he'd done. He said it was no problem and that I deserved it.

He noticed I had my Euxton Girls FC hoody on and asked if I played football and if they were my team. When I said yes he asked me all sorts of questions: Had we played that day? Did we win? What position did I play? He was really chatty. The whole story ended up on Facebook and Twitter. It got lots of likes and a lot of people commented saying what a kind thing it was of Seáni to do and that he is a top man. It really was a great experience.

Photo courtesy of Jamie Banks.

GARY MOUNSEY
MEMORABILIA COLLECTOR

My Nan used to work at Kenyon's confectioners on Church Street just a few doors down from Willie Cunningham's sports shop. She told me he used to play for PNE and that I should go in and see him, so I did.

I must've been about nine years old. He was a real gent and gave me a box full of old programmes and said he once played in a cup final.

It was about that time a neighbour of ours called David started taking me on Deepdale. I fell in love with Alex Bruce, Ricky Thomson and Mike 'walks on water' Elwiss, and I've had a deep love for the club ever since. Later in life, I was lucky to meet those early heroes of mine through the PNE Former Players Association. I was good friends with Leo Gornall (now sadly passed) who played for PNE reserves in the late 50s. Leo introduced me to the Association and also took me to the fabled allotment. Many times I took bacon and sausages down to Tommy Thompson and Les Dagger to listen to their stories! I once also visited a rest home in Bamber Bridge on the off-chance of getting Joe Dunn's autograph and spent an hour listening to his stories about football and how he and Tommy Doc used to own the Olympic Café in town. It was a remarkable hour.

I'd say the old games in the 3rd and 4th Divisions are my most memorable. I remember going to watch Wrexham v Peterborough in the last game of the 77-78 season. Peterborough needed a win to go up but only managed a draw and so we got promoted to Division 2. Then there's Hartlepool away in the Sherpa Van Trophy 1988 – a Tuesday night, torrential rain, 2,000 PNE fans and me. I climbed up on floodlight to watch the game and we all ran onto the pitch after we'd won and got covered in mud. What a night!

I have a wide collection of North End memorabilia and I love the buzz of finding something different to add to it. My most treasured items are probably an 1889 season ticket member card and Sir Tom Finney's cap. The member card is bound in leather and was issued from the Unicorn

Hotel where Fred Dewhurst (the secretary of PNE and Invincibles' double-winning captain) was the landlord. I bought Sir Tom's cap at an auction to raise money for Alzheimer's, and I had the pleasure of him coming to my house to sign the photo of him handing it to me. I also have Bud Maxwell's 1938 Cup Final Winners medal which I treasure. It's solid gold and only eleven were issued.

There are still many items I'd love to have, like an Invincibles League or Cup medal, a shirt or medal from any of North End's cup finals, or the twelve programmes I need to complete my collection of every home and away programme from 1946/47 to the 1999/2000 season. I'll keep looking!

What does supporting PNE mean to me? It's about having a bond. I can honestly say that bond has helped me through life. Following PNE can make you mad, sad or happy. But whether you're winning or losing, bottom of the 4th or challenging for the play-offs, the bond is always there. You might stop going on for a few games, but you'll always return.

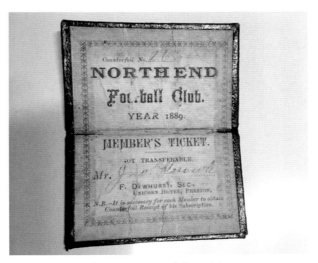

Insert photo courtesy of Gary Mounsey.

JO HARWOOD
1970s PNE LADIES SHIRT

I have a shirt from the PNE Supporters Club Ladies team from the early 1970s. You couldn't get replica shirts in those days so my Mum just bought an ordinary white football shirt and sewed the badge on.

I don't know where she got the badge from. It's one of the lovely old-style badges. My Sister, Clare, wore the shirt as a mascot for the team when we first started out around 1972, nearly fifty years ago! She's in the photo holding the ball and I'm sat behind her.

The photo appeared in the paper and was taken outside the Supporters Club which was the old club shop. We used to meet up there, get changed, go and train on Moor Park and then afterwards we'd go in the Supporters Club for a drink. They were great days!

I played for the Ladies team but Clare never did, however she does now play with us in the PNE Walking Football teams.

I've actually got a Losers FA Cup Final medal for PNE Ladies. It was the FA Cup for women and, unfortunately, we got beat 1-0 by St Helens. We played the final at Enfield because, at the time, women were still banned from playing on league grounds.

I started my football career as a striker but worked my way back and ended up at centre-half.

'Along with the FA Cup Final, another highlight is being picked for the very first official England Women's squad which I think was in the 1971-72 season.'

In 1972, North End were drawn at home to play Man United on the 5th February in the 4th round of the FA Cup. We would've struggled to get tickets as they went on sale at seven in the morning so my friend and I skipped off school to go and queue at 7am. We told the school we were ill and, low and behold, a photo of us queuing appeared in The Evening Post that night. It was fairly obvious we weren't sick!

Everybody in school saw it. The teachers all saw it, but they weren't too bothered. We were in sixth form then and the teachers just said you didn't miss much really. As for my Dad, being a football fan, he completely understood!

(Black and white photo: PNE Supporters Club Ladies Team, circa 1972)

Insert photo courtesy of Jo Harwood

JOHN BILLINGTON
PNE-STYLED SCOOTER

My PNE-styled bike is a 1972 Lambretta GP scooter which was modified in 2009 with an Aprilia engine by local lad, Frank Sanderson, a scooter manufacturer and avid PNE Fan.

I got the bike for my 50th birthday and collected it a year early. Since then, I've added different badges and graphics to it over time just to personalise it. The Sir Tom Finney artwork is by the famous caricaturist, Bob Bond, who kindly gave me permission to use the images.

It's proved quite popular over the years and has featured at shows, appeared in scootering magazines and calendars, and has even been requested at weddings for the bride and groom to sit on! But it's not just for show. I actually use it for work and I also ride it with the Preston Wildcats Scooter Club.

On occasion, I like taking it to Blackpool to show off and ride it along the prom. It was on show at The National Football Museum when it opened at Deepdale and many fans had their photos taken with it, including Derek Shaw. People will recall seeing it in the windows of Finney's Cafe as I left it there when I took it off the road during winter.

'Sir Tom's signature on the scooter is the real thing, and how it came about was quite bizarre.'

I'd not had it that long when, on the way home from work, I stopped at The Evening Post's offices at Eastway to grab a copy of the paper. When I arrived inside, who was there but Sir Tom himself!

He was with his chauffeur handing over loads of books and gifts to be used as raffle prizes so I went over and said, 'Excuse me, I'm really sorry, Tom, but would there be any chance of you signing something for me?'

'Of course I will! I'll sign anything.' he said.

I said, 'can I bring it in?'

'What is it?'

So I went outside and wheeled the scooter into the foyer of The Evening Post's offices.

'I've never seen anything like this!' he said. Well, the place came to life. People started appearing from nowhere and, the next thing I knew, photographs were being taken of Sir Tom with the bike. The whole episode was featured in The Post.

After signing the bike, Sir Tom was concerned the signature would wash off in the rain but I told him no, that's going home right now and I'm going to lacquer it, and I did. I put ten layers of lacquer over it! It was a fantastic chance meeting and it's great to have. I could never sell it. I'll never get rid of it.

JOHN JACKSON
PNE COLLECTOR

I've got a letter from Downing Street. I wrote to them a year before Sir Tom was knighted telling them it was about time he was made a Sir and they actually replied thanking me for my suggestion and saying it was being taken into consideration. A year later he was knighted!

My main collection of PNE stuff is displayed in what I call my PNE room and in it is my Finney wall with all things Sir Tom. A while back, I got a shirt signed by Sir Tom and my Wife, Melanie – who said she'd never marry a man who was into football – bought me a frame for it. I had other things already but when I got that it just sparked something and my collecting kicked off from there. I started looking up PNE memorabilia and Tom Finney items. I bought his autograph book, a signed cap he won for England and some old shin pads that he used to advertise. I once met Sir Tom at the supporters' club. I'd won something in a raffle and he shook my hand. I never saw him play. I wish I had. You wouldn't be able to stop him these days with the boots they wear now, and you wouldn't be able to buy him either. He'd be up there with Messi.

I mainly go on eBay for items and check on there most nights. I bought an old PNE rattle on there for 25 quid. If you took that to the ground today, you'd get arrested. I've signed boots by Garner, Tom Clarke's armband, programmes, commemorative plates, badges, medals, photos, cigarette cards, flags, scarves, figures, tickets and loads of plastic grass. As you can see, I'm PNE mad and even had me Son christened Paul Neil Edward – PNE!

I first watched North End in the 1964 Cup Final at Wembley on telly. I didn't support any team before then, but I picked North End that day and that were it. I was born in Knott End, so I could've been other end, I could've been a Lasher! I didn't know at the time, but me Dad was a North Ender as well, so it went in family.

When I was about fifteen or sixteen, I got circled in a programme. They used to circle a fan from a photo of the Kop or the Town End and if you won you got to sit next to the bench and meet all players. It was United we played and we lost 1-0 in the Cup. Georgie Best, Sadler and all them lot were playing. North End had a player called Clive 'Chippy' Clark and it was like he was on train tracks – whoosh, straight down the wing! A right skinny little fella but he couldn't half move.

In those days, I used to catch a bus from Knott End to Poulton then a Ribble bus from Poulton to Preston and walk all the way to the ground. Going back, I'd get to Poulton and have to catch the 7 o'clock bus to get home. It was a long day. And remember that day we had no floodlights and played in the afternoon, when Mel Tottoh came on in the second half? Oh, I got soaked walking back; it was pouring down.

I started off going on the Kop then later I went on the West Stand. I liked it on there. I took me Daughter, Chelsey on there when she was only eight weeks old. I'll never forget it, we won 5-1 and I forgot I had her strapped to my front after about the third goal! Oh, them were the days.

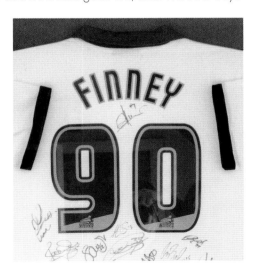

RICHARD GIDDINS
SPION KOP SIGN

It was PNE v Walsall, the last game of the 1996/97 season. A sunny day, party atmosphere, full house and the last time the famous Spion Kop would be used before a new stand was put in its place.

We left the ground later than normal and, when the crowd had dispersed, found ourselves – me and my two Brothers, Edmund and Patrick – outside the Kop turnstiles. A few people were still around and, knowing the stand was going to be demolished, we decided to 'save' the sign for posterity, and from destruction. Patrick got on Edmund's shoulders, basically ripped it from the wall, and passed it down to me.

'A passing policeman gave us a wink, and carried on his way.'

Some fellow supporters congratulated us on gaining a fine memento from the famous old stand and Dad couldn't believe we'd brought back such a large sign to fit in his small car. It was always getting in there though. The sign now resides at my Brother's house. Inside, not out!

Loads of funny incidents have happened during my time supporting the Whites. Years ago, one Easter when Nobby Stiles was manager, I was at home not doing much and decided to phone PNE. I asked to speak to Nobby and, unbelievably, was put through to him! I said, 'Hello. Good luck for the next game.' I was only about twelve, pretty naive and shy, and I remember him asking why I wasn't at school. I explained it was a Holy day. He asked if I'd been to church yet and said he needed to go himself later on.

I also phoned Graham Bell once. Knowing he was from Oldham, I scanned the directory for a Mr G. Bell in Oldham and, miraculously, the one I chose turned out to be him! We had a great conversation about PNE, and as the call was coming to an end, Graham asked if I'd like tickets for the next home game. 'Yes! Six please!'

He laughed and said he could manage three which we received from him outside the players entrance the following Saturday.

However, my most amazing incident involving a telephone call happened one evening in September 1981. I was fourteen and Dad had been telling me about a game Bill Shankly played in which ended something like 5-5 or 7-7. I'm not fully sure of the score, but Dad suggested I write to Mr Shankly and ask him about the game, which I did. I'd not got a reply and had long forgotten about it when one evening I was lying on the front-room floor watching Coronation Street when the phone rang. From the other room Mum shouts, 'Richard! You're wanted on the phone. It's Bill Shankly.' I was flabbergasted and again, due to my age and feeling in awe, only had a brief conversation with him.

He apologised for not replying sooner and said he'd decided to call rather than have me wait for a letter. He then told me about his time at PNE before my Mum demanded she talk to him! They were chatting for a good half hour, reminiscing not just about football but about all things Preston – the area, the old days and so on. It was brilliant to listen to, even though we could only hear one side of the conversation. That memory is even more precious knowing that Bill sadly passed a few days later.

Mum and Dad were massive PNE fans and we all followed suit. For me, no other team matters. From the first minute I stepped on Deepdale, to this present day, no other team could have given me such joy, sadness, frustration, happiness and anger. I wouldn't go through all that for just any old team!

Photo courtesy of Richard Giddins (L to R): Patrick, Richard, & Edmund Giddins.

STUART CHADWICK
HARRIS MUSEUM, VISITOR SERVICES SUPERVISOR

I t's not every day you get to hold the 1941 War Cup trophy aloft as part of your job. As a lifelong North Ender, it's a real privilege for me to work amongst these items, and the Harris Museum's North End collection is very special to me.

I've many favourite items but the Football League War Cup does stand out. It's basically the last major trophy they won. The tournament ran during the Second World War as normal football competition was suspended due to hostilities. The final went to two games and, after a 1-1 draw at Wembley, North End beat a very good Arsenal side 2-1 in the replay at Ewood Park thanks to two goals from Bobbie Beattie. By winning the War Cup, North End became the first team to complete a wartime league and cup double after having already won the Northern Regional League. Another first for our proud club! Captain Tom Smith collected the trophy just three years after collecting the FA Cup at Wembley. As reward for winning the trophy, the players each received five wartime savings certificates.

There were some famous PNE names in that War Cup team. One of those was a young Tom Finney; his Football Writers' Footballer of the Year trophy from 1957 is another prized item in our collection. Sir Tom first won the trophy in 1954 and, by picking it up again three years later, became the first player to win it twice. It stands just above a pair of his boots; those, and a few other items, are on display courtesy of the Finney family.

Another PNE family who have kindly provided for our cabinet are the Kelly's who have lent us Alan Kelly Senior's 1964 FA Cup Final shirt and runners-up medal. Alan was injured towards the end of the game with the score at 2-2. The ref restarted before Alan could recover and West Ham went on to win, but it was a great run by PNE who were in the old Division Two at the time, and that team is considered one of our finest ever.

Other items of interest include a medal awarded to Invincible and double-winning captain, Fred Dewhurst, a

piece of plastic pitch and a casket presented to former PNE Chairman, William Ord in 1921.

But one object that always catches people's eye is an earthenware Staffordshire teapot! It was made in 1938 to commemorate North End's FA Cup win and is displayed away from the North End collection in our Ceramics and Glass gallery.

We get many North End fans coming through the doors here and it's always nice to meet them. I always enjoy chatting with fellow fans about the club and it's a pleasure to present the collection to them if they haven't already seen it. Hopefully the collection will continue to grow and remain a fitting tribute to our proud club.

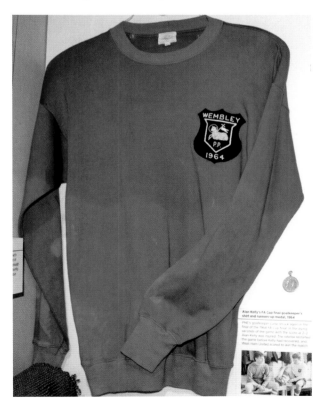

Alan Kelly's FA Cup final goalkeeper's shirt and runners-up medal, 1964

THE GENTRY
PROUD PRESTON NORTH END FC
PRESTON NORTH END
INVINCIBLES
In A League Of Their Own
The Nose Bag
SOULS
Fans' Panel

HISTORIANS

+

SCRIBES

DAVE SEDDON
SPORTS WRITER AT THE LANCASHIRE POST

I'm fortunate my job is covering my hometown club who I've supported all my life. Preston North End mean so much to me. It's just been part of my life from when I was a nipper. It was non-negotiable.

If you went to watch football then you went to North End. My Dad's a massive fan and both my Grandads were.

First football shirt was a white silky Adidas one, no sponsor, no badge, just PNEFC in italics and stripes down the sleeves. I couldn't get the replica away kit so I remember my Mum went to Merigold's and just bought us a plain yellow kit. No markings on it, but to me that was my North End away kit.

I think the first game I went on was about '76 at home to Mansfield. My Mum, Dad, Brother and me'self all went to the game. Mum went knowing I'd probably get bored and she'd take me home. I was about four or five. I lasted an hour then my Mum took me home!

The following season we all got season tickets. We used to sit in the old Pavilion stand towards the Town End. It was the promotion season under Nobby Stiles so, for a young kid, it was a great introduction. North End fans used to sing 'E-I-E-I-O when we get promotion this is what we sing, Nobby is a king . . .'

The last game of that season we drew 2-2 with Shrewsbury and there was a big pitch invasion. I was looking down from the Pavilion thinking, *wow look at all those people on the pitch!* But because we only drew, Peterborough could catch us if they won a few days later at Wrexham.

That was the bank holiday Monday and there was a reserve match at Deepdale kicking off an hour earlier at 2pm. So me my Dad and my Brother went to watch this reserve match then afterwards everyone crowded into the old Guild Club bar in the Pavilion and waited for news to come through from Wrexham. It was Radio Blackburn in those days and it came through that Peterborough had only drawn and so North End went up in third place on goal difference.

'Quite a lot of the players were there and the champagne corks started popping!'

I got a load of autographs and an empty champagne bottle that I took home. I was only a kid, but they're really good memories. Not bad for my first full season!

From a reporting point of view, the Play-off Final was something else. I got to Wembley full of nerves, but to take the lead after two minutes and to be 3-0 up by half-time was just fantastic. It was a 5:30 kick-off on a Sunday and we had 28 pages to get through ready for the Monday issue which was to be printed about 2am – that was the challenge. We enjoyed the game so much but, as soon as the final whistle went, it were heads down and straight to the interview area. We were trying to get players out of the dressing room to interview and they were bouncing around spraying each other with champagne! You just wanted them out as quickly as possible. It was a tight deadline at the end but we got there.

I got this job as PNE reporter in 2009. The best thing about it is that I'm being paid to watch football. Of course, there's pressures and it's not perfect all the time, but for someone to say go and watch football on a Saturday afternoon when other folk are paying thirty quid for it then yeah, you're in a privileged profession.

Twitter: @Sedds_lep

GAIL NEWSHAM
DICK, KERR LADIES AUTHOR AND HISTORIAN

On Friday 22nd December 2017, thanks to a fantastic group of people and sponsors, we unveiled a six-metre-high granite memorial at Deepdale to celebrate the remarkable achievements of the legendary Dick, Kerr Ladies.

The occasion marked their centenary year and followed twenty-five years of my efforts of promoting and telling their story.

I grew up in Preston just a stone's throw from the Dick, Kerr works on Strand Road. For more years than I can recall, this factory was at the heart of the town and provided jobs for thousands of families for generations. Even to this day, many people have relatives who worked there and they all have their own stories to tell and, as long ago as I can remember, I do recall hearing tales of a football team called the Dick, Kerr Ladies. 'It's very fitting to have the memorial at Deepdale as there is great history between the Dick, Kerr Ladies and Preston North End.'

On Christmas Day 1917, 10,000 spectators attended Deepdale to watch the ladies play their first game which they won 4-0. It was the start of an incredible journey and through that first match they raised £600 for wounded soldiers receiving treatment at the Moor Park Military Hospital. Today, that's the equivalent of almost £50,000.

The team received valuable coaching from several North End players who worked at the Dick, Kerr factory on Strand Road and quickly earned a reputation for being a brilliant footballing side. The PNE players who helped with coaching included Johnny Morley, Billy Grier, Jack Warner and perhaps the most celebrated of the 'Old Invincibles' team, Bob Holmes. In fact, it was Bob Holmes who was whitewashing brown footballs so that they could be seen from all corners of the ground when the ladies played in the first football night match at Deepdale in 1920. Of course, with no floodlights at the stadium back then the night sky above Deepdale was lit up by two anti-aircraft search lights kindly loaned by the War Office with permission from the Secretary of State for War, Mr Winston Churchill.

The Dick, Kerr Ladies, who later became Preston Ladies, achieved an unbeaten run of 320 matches and raised the equivalent of £10m for war-related charities. Their amazing successes inevitably led to comparisons with North End's famous Invincibles but sadly, in December 1921, the FA imposed a ban on women's football that would last for fifty years. Little was known about them until my book was originally published in 1994. Until then, there was no official record of the team.

'No one knew just how big their story was or in fact who the ladies actually were.'

For me, to see the memorial close to 'The Splash' is very special. Sir Tom and Joan Whalley were childhood pals and could often be seen playing football together on Waverley Park. The young Tom dreamed of playing football for PNE and Joan for DKL. They both played on the right wing and they both achieved their dreams. Sir Tom was inducted into the Football Hall of Fame in 2002 and Joan in 2007.

Interview includes extracts taken from Gail's book: In A League Of Their Own! The Dick, Kerr Ladies 1917-1965.

Visit: www.dickkerrladies.com

IAN RIGBY
AUTHOR AND OFFICIAL PNE HISTORIAN

TO THE MEMORY OF
THE PRESTON NORTH END EX-FOOTBALLERS,
INCLUDING RESERVE TEAM PLAYERS AND
REGISTERED AMATEURS,
WHO DIED DURING THE GREAT WAR 1914 - 1918

PNE is probably in my blood. I was born within a mile of Deepdale, lived within a mile from Deepdale and got married in St Gregory the Great's church opposite Deepdale.

My Mum and Aunty used to go on before the war and it was them that introduced me to the North End in all honesty. My Aunty worked at the Royal Infirmary and used to bring me home programmes as the club gave a few out for patients to read whilst listening to the games on Hospital Radio.

'As a kid, I used to go and watch North End training whenever I could.'

And my first real memory is of attending Tom Finney's testimonial game.

In 1981, a good book came out called *100 Years at Deepdale* to commemorate the Club's Centenary. I asked the question, 'When was the Club's first game?' And the answer was, 'We don't know' I found out that it was in 1878 and have looked at our early history ever since!

In 1983, the PNE programme editor asked for ideas for the forthcoming seasons programme. I wrote in with some suggestions and she said, 'Very good. Can you write them?' Well, English was not my best subject at school but I said I would give it a go and that's how it started. Later, my friend and co-author, Mike Payne and I decided to try and put all the info we had into book form to coincide with PNE's 100th season, and hence produced our *Proud Preston* book, which I will add, we are very proud of. That sold around 3,500 copies and sold out! We then updated and reprinted it a few years later as *Loud and Proud*.

My position as Official PNE Historian came about after my Daughter wrote a letter one Christmas to then Chairman, Derek Shaw. I used to travel to away games

with the LEP sports reporter, Brian Ellis, and he'd tagged me as 'North End's unofficial historian' so my Daughter asked Derek to make it official!

My main role is answering any questions the club get asked about old players, for example by people researching their family trees. I never fail to answer one of those queries as the family will, more often than not, know something about the player, family-wise, that I will not.

My role of Historian mingles with my role as Secretary of The PNE Former Players' Association. I was once interviewed for an article in the North End programme and mentioned I would like the club to form a Former Players' Association. Little did I realise I'd be one of the four guys to set it up and running. Two years after that article, the Association came into fruition and that was, unbelievably, in January 1998.

Since then, I've met many former players who I would never had met in my life, and become good friends with many too. I've helped organise reunions for the 1964 FA Cup Final squad, for which five West Ham players also attended, a reunion for the 1970-71 Third Division Champions team, one for the 1960 PNE Youth Cup final team, and so on. Other events that take pride of place are arranging Sir Tom's 80th and 90th birthday parties and Tommy Thompson's 80th birthday bash. Many golf days have come and gone, along with our well-attended Sportsman's Dinners.

I am always researching something about the Club but probably my proudest moment – having researched all the information – was unveiling the War Memorial outside the ground which commemorates the 21 ex-North Enders who gave their lives during The Great War.

Photo courtesy of Ian Rigby

JOHN ROPER

PNE FANS PANEL WRITER

My Mother's family were all North Enders, then my Uncle brought my Dad to Deepdale in 1950 to watch Tom Finney and that were it, end of story. I was seven when Dad first brought me; we lost 1-0 to Bristol City in '67.

We stood on the old Spion Kop on the bit that came round to the Pavilion Paddock. We always stood there, come hail, rain or snow, we'd be on that corner and it was always the same people. There were some characters. It was a great introduction.

Back in the 90s, right after the John Beck era, we were playing Lincoln away. Me and my mate were the first two North Enders inside the ground at Sincil Bank, so we go for a pie and it's got written up 'Pies: 60p'. The guy behind the counter goes, 'You from Preston, what can I do you for?'

'A pie and a coffee please.'

Then whilst serving the coffee he asks, 'How many you bringing today?'

I said, 'Oh, about 1,500.' With this, he picked up a cloth, rubbed the 60p out on the pies and put £1!

'You can have yours for 60p but don't tell a soul!' You could see the pound signs light up in this fella's eyes. Fantastic!

Gary Peters was in charge then, and I think that was Beckham's last game.

The writing goes back to the 2000-2001 season when The Evening Post started their fans panel, and I've been doing it ever since. I usually write 400-600 words. Some games, you struggle to get 400 whilst others you could go on and on. I'm not a natural writer, but I've probably done about 900 games since I started so I'm well practiced.

People want the details: who played well? Who had a stinker? What were the goals? And so on. I'm a short story match reporter. I'm not doing a Dave Seddon, I wouldn't try that!

My blog is the write-up in its purest form, the uncut version. I also do a match preview and add a bet for the weekend. I think I'm more tactically aware after doing so many games. You get to know the different managers, how they like to set up their teams and when they like to use subs, but it's always just how I saw it. Someone might come up to me at a game and say, 'What a load of crap you wrote!' And that's fair enough, it's all opinions. I get a lot of banter which is really good. It's brought me a lot of fun.

I've always been associated with PNE. I left junior school in '71, and around the school yard there were United kits, Leeds, Rovers, and one lad in a white top with the blue square badge – me.

Over my 52 years, we've had some great days and some bad, but I've learnt to get over the bad quickly. I remember being away to non-league Scarborough in the Cup in '75. We're 2-1 up and there's two foot of snow on the ground. Then Scarborough score twice including a last-minute goal to win 3-2. Unbelievable!

I get frustrated with what Sky has done to football and the missing generation of fans we should have had, but the frustration is wiped away when the ball goes in the net. There's nothing else like it. It's given me unbridled joy and the depth of despair. Yes, it's only football, but it's not football, it's Preston North End. It's deep in my heart and in my soul, unfortunately!

jrpneblog.tumblr.com

KEITH HARRISON
AUTHOR OF *NORTH END SOULS*

My earliest North End memory is being taken from my Nan's house on Greenlands estate in Ribbleton and walked down Blackpool Road to see Bobby Charlton play for us.

I remember it mostly for being a long way for a six year old, especially as I had little legs at the time, like Daryl Horgan. Of course it's a bit vague, and I was too young to realise how lucky I was — I'd just got off Greenlands without being mugged!

Nan was North End through and through. Later on, she couldn't get to the games but she'd sit on her back step, smoking a fag, listening for the cheers wafting in from Deepdale and seeing how long it took Red Rose to play their 'GOAL ACTION FROM DEEPDALE!' jingle on the wireless.

To be fair, by the time I started high school and going on regularly with my mates, she wasn't missing much. The late 1970s/early 1980s was hardly a purple patch, but it didn't really matter by then, we were on a game. Deepdale was better than Wembley. It still is, to me. The back of the vast Spion Kop was ours. Young lads jumping around like House of Pain. Plenty of room until it rained when everyone huddled under the shelter.

I remember my mate saying, 'I bet this is what it's like being on the REAL Kop.' 'What do you mean?' I said, 'this IS the real Kop!' Afterwards, we'd leg it up Skeffington Road, see if Rounds had any pies left and try not to miss the red Ribble bus back to Grimsargh. The Corpy one only went as far as Gamull. Nightmare. Crowds weren't great. By 84/85 we averaged about 4,000 for home games but there was great camaraderie and I still see plenty of those old lads on thgames now. Some I've 'known' for decades without ever putting a name to them. It's just a nod of acknowledgement. Yes mate, we were THERE.

Scunthorpe at home, Aldershot away, the Orient Express, 53 Miles West of Venus: things that require no further explanation to those who know. Same with Ronnie's Rocket.

I still go on some games with most of the lads from back then and, to be honest, little has changed. We're older and supposedly wiser, but our love for PNE is stronger than ever and binds us even closer as the years go by.

We spend many happy hours discussing Willie Naughton and his support group, Peter Sayer, John Slowey, Mark Rodgers, 'I'd rather have Ted Rodgers!' and 3-2-1 . . . the link is Mel Tottoh. Or it could be 'that day in Scunny', 'that night in Norwich', 'that gay club in Milton Keynes' (don't ask, don't tell), that goal by Gregan, the unerring forehead of Gary Swann, the craptitude of Richard Chaplow, Dale Rudge's tash, a long-standing hatred of David Johnson, lazy gits galore, Gary Bennett's teeth, Barry Siddall's pumps, JT, Grezza, Our Kid, their kids, Ryan Kidd. It's all connected.

It's been there all our lives and it never ends. It's why my wife wearily says, 'All roads lead to Deepdale'.

It's because they do.
It's part of us.
And we're part of it.
Maybe the biggest part.
Because it's us, the fans, that beat at its heart.
That give it real meaning.
Because it DOES mean something.
It does. It really bloody does.
We're it and it is us.
The club is the body, a thing of sheer beauty, and we, my friends, are the North End souls.
Now, there's a good title for a book . . .

www.northendsouls.com   @northendsouls

MARTIN ATHERTON
PNE STATISTICIAN

When Sir Tom Finney held a charity match for his Alzhemers charity, I was asked to chaperone some of the older ex-professionals, and I remember walking in front of the Town End with Tommy Thompson.

I said to him, 'You scored a few goals here.' and he said, 'You know, when Tom put ball across on yer head, it would be an insult not to put it in net!' I thought it was a lovely thing to say. He was so matter of fact about it.

I remember the last away game of the season against Fulham in '71. We went to London by coach. Left at something like six in the morning from Starch House Square. I was fifteen and my parents just let me go. Fortunately, we tagged up with an older lad who was probably only about nineteen.

We got to Victoria Coach Station and the driver said, 'We leave at 11:30pm!' and that was it. He didn't take us to the ground. We'd never even thought of how we were going to get to the ground! Anyway, we ended up on the underground and Sir Alf Ramsey was in our carriage sat across from us. It turned out he was going to Fulham to present them with the trophy because, if they won, they'd win the Third Division title, but they didn't, we won 1-0! Ricky Heppolette with a diving header. And then we beat Rotherham on the Monday and leapfrogged Fulham to become Champions instead. But Alf Ramsey, we were like rabbits in the headlights.

'Is that Alf Ramsey?'
'Yes, that's Alf Ramsey!'
'No chance!'
'Yes, it is, that's Alf Ramsey.'

And so we went on whispering. Not one of us dared speak to him! And then he walked down to the ground with us. Sir Alf, England Manager, walked through Putney Bridge Station, through the park all the way to the ground.

It was like we were stalking him, or he was stalking us!

After the game, we went round to the team coach to see if we could get any autographs, and Ricky Heppolette's wife was there passing around this bottle of champagne and we were all drinking out of it but it tasted horrible to me to be honest. Then we went off straight back into Central London. We weren't bothered about doing anything touristy, we weren't tourists, we just wanted to find a pub with a TV because we knew North End were going to be on Match of the Day. After a long search, we finally found the one pub in London with a TV in 1971 and that TV wasn't working!

Thanks to Dave Russell and Brian Gray, I began the role of Club Statistician in 1996 along with my mate, Tony. In 2009, Tony stopped and I just carried on so I've been doing it for over 23 years now. I trained as a historian at university and, before each game, I always do some research.

'It's a discipline.'

You check your sources and you don't just check one, you cross reference, then you put it out there and share it. Share it, don't keep it! I go into the press room before games to pass on any notes and feed any relevant stats or anniversaries to the media team. I love doing it.

Players come and go, fans come and go, but the club is always there and this history keeps its story alive. It's a connection between people, passing on stories through families and friends. I feel so honoured and privileged to do this, and get more from it than I give.

PETER HOLME

NFM COLLECTIONS OFFICER AND CURATOR

In 2009, the National Football Museum had to close in Preston due to a lack of money, really. The Football Foundation had funded it, or partly funded it for six years, and made it a free entry museum, but they suddenly said they couldn't fund it anymore.

So the Museum was suddenly £600,000 short which meant it had to close. In the meantime, Manchester Council had shown an interest in using the Urbis building and promised to give some funding, initially £2 million per year, so that was the main reason. It was dying in Preston without the funding which was a real shame.

When it opened in Manchester, I offered to remain in Preston to help look after the archive which is still open here in Preston for researchers and stuff. People may think it's completely closed, but it isn't. We have this second site here in Deepdale where we store all the objects not on display in Manchester. This is a purpose-built storage facility set to the ideal temperature and humidity.

'We've got over 35,000 objects, including books and archive material and, of those, only 2,000 are on display, so there's a lot in the reserve collection!'

We're open on Mondays and Tuesdays for any visitors looking to do some research. Visitors can include amateur historians, authors researching for books or students and historians from universities. Everyone is welcome and we meet all sorts of people from this country and abroad.

We have a number of items from Sir Tom Finney's family and they are very dear to us. When the Museum closed, they requested some of them be kept here in safe storage which we were very happy to do.

One of his Player of the Year awards is in Manchester, and there are more items from the Finney collection on display in the Harris Museum and UCLan's Sir Tom Finney Sports Centre. Plus, we still have some items here in storage belonging to the collection and of course, if the family ever wish to do a display, they're available.

The PNE collection itself is much wider and includes minute books, gate receipt books, wage books from the 30s and 40s, team sheets from the 50s and a wide range of photographs. It's a huge collection and its lucky these things haven't been thrown away.

One of my favourite PNE items is a coloured fixture card from 1883 showing all North End's games for that season. It displays the players wearing red and white stripes and shows Major Sudell, the manager and driving force behind them becoming the Ivincibles. All thegames are friendlies as there was no League back then, and so in this one item you can see a lot about the early history of football and PNE.

But of all the items, my favourite has to be the original FA Cup trophy from the 1890s. It's not as big as the present FA Cup but it's a beautiful piece of Victorian silverware and the most valuable item of football memorabilia ever sold at auction. Unfortunately PNE didn't win that actual cup in 1889. The one they won was stolen, but this one is based on it and was used afterwards, so it does sort of take you back to that period when PNE claimed it to clinch the first ever double!

WHITES

IN

EXILE

ANGUS McGUNNIGLE
NORWAY

I moved to Norway in December '96 just a couple of weeks after that glorious Friday night demolition of Blackpool. In the beginning, my Dad used to send me match reports from the LEP, and I also arranged a deal with George Hodgson to post me videos of games on VHS.

This was great in theory but sitting at home alone watching North End lose on penalties at Hartlepool in the Auto Windscreens Shield, three weeks after the event, wasn`t always that thrilling in practice.

One Saturday afternoon in Bergen, I somehow managed to tune in to Radio Lancs. I couldn`t believe it. I sent them an excited email shortly afterwards requesting the frequency but they replied saying it was a fluke! The internet, Ryanair and, more recently, iFollow have made things far easier now, although watching matches live actually makes me even more homesick.

One of my favourite memories following PNE is seeing a queue of lads delivering pieces of plastic pitch to the cloakroom attendant in Tokes, after that incredible match against Torquay in '94.

Mansfield away in '87 is an important match for me as I started a lifelong friendship, but my favourite away game has to be Hartlepool in '88 – the Sherpa Van Trophy Northern Area semi-final. It was 80s football at its very best: a packed terrace on a wet Tuesday night, horrendously muddy pitch, unfriendly locals, the lure of Wembley before it lost its aura, that iconic yellow Garratts kit . . . A lad on a floodlight and pure passion and singing. The crush leaving the ground was so bad I was carried down a staircase without my feet touching the steps – a really weird experience. My ski hat, perched on the back of my head in the style of the time, slipped off and I couldn`t lift my arms to catch it.

I`ve definitely done some daft things watching North End tho'. Back in 2014, I arrived in Colchester about 9:30-ish from Oslo, met up with the lads and had a few drinks. Alcohol is a third of the price in England compared to Scandinavia so I must have got a bit carried away. Anyway, on the half hour mark, Preston won a corner and, for some reason, I bragged to the lad next to me that I'd run on the pitch if we scored from it. I had zero intention of doing so but within seconds, Tom Clarke had nodded in Gally's cross. I was too embarrassed to go back on my word so I hurdled the advertising hoarding and slid on both knees by the touchline. It felt quite good actually, but obviously I was ejected immediately and given a ticking off by the local constabulary. In fairness, they directed me to the nearest pub and declined to press charges which was fortunate given where I live.

Anyway, I had a couple more pints and managed to nick back in for the final five mins having swapped hats with one of my pals. Probably the worst aspect of it all was wandering through Stansted airport with two massive brown muddy skid marks on my black cords.

My Mum still lives in Penwortham and I'm looking forward to returning to Preston once both my kids are up and running. Without getting too sentimental, supporting PNE does mean a lot. It provides me with a link to my past; reminds me of my Dad and has given me many of the best friendships I have. In an increasingly atomised society, following North End remains one of the few areas left that engenders a sense of community and local pride. It gives a huge amount of meaning to so many Prestonians, and long may it continue.

Photo courtesy of Angus McGunnigle.
(L to R): Angus, Peter.

GARY HARRIS-NEWSHAM
TASMANIA, AUSTRALIA

Following PNE from afar has its plus points as, thanks to iFollow, I can usually watch 95% of the games. It's funny, I ring my mum back in Preston and let her know I'm watching the game and she's sat at home having to listen to it on Radio Lancashire.

Me and my Wife (who is Australian) got married in 2004 and we did three years in the UK before moving out here to a little place called Karoola, which is 25 km NE of Launceston. The nearest PNE fan to us I know is approximately 140 miles away in Hobart. The down side, until recently, has been not having anyone to watch the matches with as kick off times can vary from 9pm till 5am. Since Covid though, a great group has been going on Facebook called the Virtual Supporters Group and through this I've been watching matches live with other fans. We all use iFollow whilst chatting through Zoom. We've fans from Malta, Edinburgh and some local Prestonians from Lostock Hall. I also chat to a few other fans around Australia on a page called Whites Downunder.

'My first PNE memory is the Friday night game at home to Northampton in the 86/87 season. Nothing beats a game under the lights at Deepdale!'

They were top, we were second, and there was a crowd of 16,456. I went into the West Stand Paddock and made my way to the front. The atmosphere was just amazing and I loved it.

A lot of my favourite memories are of working in different bars in the Pavilion Stand. Great moments like meeting David Beckham when he came on loan as a young lad, and Kenny Dalglish who was a great gent and even bought the bar staff a drink. At the time, I was helping out in the Players Bar which was behind the gym and was more like a corridor than a bar. One day, when North End played Rotherham, I was on the door when two gents walked up and said they'd been told to come to the bar and would be let in. They said they were the Chuckle Brothers, Paul and Barry. I hadn't a clue who they were, but after chatting to a Rotherham player, we let them in.

I've got a few PNE items but the one I love the most is my Matchwinner training top which I got off David Flitcroft. I used to work at Royal Mail with one of Flitcroft's mates who was also a trainee at PNE but sadly didn't make the grade. One day, I was chatting to him and David and David just gave me the training top. I loved it, as although you could buy the same one in the shop, the one David gave me also had the Matchwinner logo on the back. It's the one I'm wearing in the photo.

To me, supporting North End has been amazing and I've made some great friends along the way. I've visited lots of grounds too, often by different modes of Transport. I once did Gillingham away while on a motorbike trip to Brands Hatch, and the lovely staff in Gillingham's club shop kindly looked after my jacket and helmet while the game was on. I've also had great times with my parents, stopping at pubs with my Dad along the way to places like Chesterfield, Durham and Scunthorpe, and travelling with my Mum to West Brom and Derby away. At Derby, we nearly walked off at half-time we were playing that bad. But we all love the team, even when they have bad days. It can be frustrating but it's our team! With PNE, we are one family!

Photo credit: Gary Harris-Newsham

JEZ LEES

There were 35,400 on my first PNE match. Blackpool at home, 13th April, 1970. A 3-0 loss under the lights in which the victors went up to Division One and saw us go down to Division Three. I was just seven years old then and, by 1971, was a £5 a year season ticket holder.

I've lived in Pattaya, Thailand for eighteen years now and there's a few other North Enders out here so I'm not alone! We enjoy talking North End and telling the whole town who we are. There are also a lot of Blackpool lads and, I must admit, some of them are good mates. We enjoy plenty of banter and give each other stick any chance we get. I am happy to say there are next to no Plastics, Dingles or Pie Eaters. I guess they don't like going away, but we knew that already.

I work at an International school and all the kids I coach in and out of the school know all about PNE, that's for sure. Some now even support us so there's an ever-growing Thai Preston North End supporters club! It's really nice going into work on Monday and the kids knowing the Preston score.

Living in Thailand allows me to visit the Himalayas each year, a place I love as much as Preston. The mountains and the Sherpa people of the Solu Khumbu are magical. There's a North End scarf in a bar in the main Sherpa village, Namche Bazaar at 3,500m.

When I posted my PNE pictures from Everest in December 2019 on the Preston North End FC page, I was astounded to see it reach 400 likes. Even more rewarding were the good wishes I received from so many fellow fans.

Two years earlier, I had reached Base Camp on Christmas Day with ex-North legend, Dean Barrick. Dean and I both teach and coach football here and have become great mates.

That trip was very emotional for the both of us for our own personal reasons, and I am not ashamed to say we were both in tears at the end. In fact, some of my Mum's ashes

lie up there and, as she knew both Tom Finney and Bill Shankly amongst other players from the 50s, you might say there's a little bit of Preston up there.

My favourite PNE memory is actually an often-told story from my late Mum. She was probably about fifteen at the time and walking from the match towards her Ribbleton home. Suddenly, Bill Shankly sidles up alongside her.

'Have you been to tha game lass?' he asked.

Once Mum said yes, she said he never shut up talking football the whole way. He proceeded to drag her along to what Mum described as a temperance bar where, over two glasses of hot Vimto, he talked football to her for about the next two hours! She loved telling that tale to many friends here in Thailand so I know it well.

Preston North End is part of me, my history, my shared memories, my hometown, my mates, my roots. I have pretty much lived overseas constantly since 1989 when I left Preston to travel the world with my mate, Coups, another North Ender from Ashton. Since then, whether in Australia, Japan or now Thailand, I am and always will be a Preston North End fan and all of what that means.

Photos courtesy of Jez Lees.
Main photo (L to R): Dean Barrick, Jez Lees.

KOSTYA KORNEV
CIS INVINCIBLES

My name is Konstantin but most people call me Kostya. I was born in Krasnodar in Southern Russia. It's a real football city and, at one stage, two teams from Krasnodar played in the Russian Premier League.

I first learned of Preston from a friend who translated the news from Preston into Russian. Once, he asked me to help him and since then I've written constantly about Preston for residents of Russia and the CIS countries.

In my opinion, once you know the history of the North End, it's impossible not to root for them.

I first had the idea to create the group when I realised many other people in Russia and the CIS countries follow PNE.

'We are just a few months old and only at the beginning of our journey, but here in Russia we already have Preston North End fans in St Petersburg, Kronstadt, Samara, Yekaterinburg and Togliatti.'

Of the CIS countries, we have fans from Mogilev in Belarus, Pavlodar in Kazakhstan and Kharkiv in Ukraine.

Our page has over 425 followers. Some of us are in constant touch and we always try to watch the matches and discuss them. Unfortunately, we have never met each other but sooner or later we will definitely meet up!

We also have Instagram and Twitter accounts and through these we communicate with English fans and others from different countries.

Since following North End, the 2015 League One Play-off Final has to be my favourite memory. Defeating Swindon Town 4-0 and Jermaine Beckford's hat-trick – it was a very cool match! I must also mention our recent victory over Blackburn Rovers.

Supporting PNE in Russia can sometimes get me strange looks. I remember one day I went to a local match where there was a small crowd of about 300 people. I was wearing my Preston North End hoodie and when I passed by a six-year-old boy, he looked at me amazed and said, 'What is this, Preston?' It made me smile.

Of course, every member of our PNE fan club wants to attend a match of their favourite team, and one has already been fortunate enough to do so! I really hope that in the future, I too will make it to Preston; it would be amazing to watch North End play at Deepdale and meet up with some of the fans!

Twitter: @CISInvincibles
Instagram: cisinvinibles

Photo courtesy of Kostya Kornev.

MATT HIGGINS
NEW YORK NORTHENDERS

My Father, Mark, and Uncle Neil took me on my first game when I was about two years old and I've never looked back! When I was five years old, I was the mascot for a match against Crewe Alexandra.

I was so nervous beforehand. I actualy tripped over when running out for the warm-up!

My favourite ever PNE match has to be the play-off final second leg v Birmingham City. I still dream about it to this day so it must have anunderlining meaning. It was an amazing night.

I was a programme seller at the time so I had pitch-side access to David Healy's opener. I remember walking by the Sir Tom Finney stand where my Grandma, Dad and Brothers were all sat. I remember giving the fists up to my Dad! Then later, when Mark Rankine scored to equal the tie, I was stood on the old Paddock with my Uncle Neil and he had to stop me running onto the pitch! It's one of those that will be one for the Grandkids.

I used to play in goal for Macclesfield Town and when I finished playing, there was a coaching opportunity in the States and I took it. When I moved over here in 2006, there was no social media like today. There was no iFollow or anything like that so it was hard to follow the games, which I hated as I went to most PNE matches whilst I was in the UK.

Then my friend, Jack Kean, opened the Football Factory bar opposite the Empire State Building in NYC. It's a place which gives soccer fans a home to watch the games and now the 'New York Northenders' are an official supporters group of the bar! I started the group with by my great friend, John Ryding. We have a great time because there are so many supporters groups based out of the bar and we all become friends and have a laugh.

As the 'New York Northenders', we just meet up for the games and we're lucky enough to watch them all live. It's great for any PNE fan, or fans who happen to be just visiting New York too. If there's a game on, they are welcome to come and meet us. Just give us a shout!

In the bar, we have a signed Scott Laird shirt and a framed play-off final shirt. But most famously, we have Joe Garners signed yellow Nike boots!

Since it began, the supporters group has received great feedback. It's opened a lot of doors for everybody, and even some players have contacted us when they've been over, including Joe Garner and Scott Laird.

As for me now, I usually get back to England for at least one match per season. The most recent was against Hull City and my Daughter was a mascot! We had a great time.

Supporting North End means everything to me. Obviously, my Wife, Daniela, and our children, Oliver & Stella, think I'm crazy, but it's just what I was brought up with.

When I was playing for Macclesfield, we played against the PNE youth team on multiple occasions and I once lined up with Andy Lonergan as my opposite number 1. It was an honour for me and a dream come true as a fifteen/sixteen year old.

PNE are just in my blood and to finally see them in the Premier League, well, that would be what dreams are made of!

Twitter: @nycnorthenders

Photo courtesy of Matt Higgins.

NEIL JAMIESON
CONNECTICUT, USA

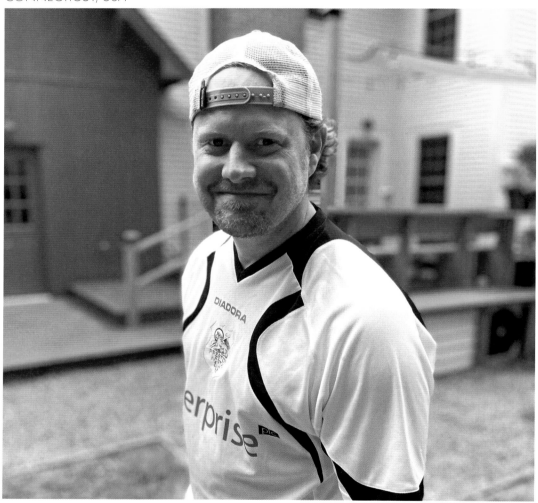

I blame it all on my Grandad! He played for North End reserves during the war and knew Tom Finney. Men of his generation all knew Finney personally of course . . . If you needed your drains sorted, Finney's company was the first call you made.

My Grandad worked for Leyland Motors as a mechanic so, during the war, he had to stay and build munitions and equipment at Leland. He was a great sportsman, mainly cricket, but he loved football and, during the war, he got his chance to pull on the reserves shirt for a couple of years.

I grew up with North End languishing around the lower leagues – some pretty rough times. Tickets were easy to come by though and it was normally a fun, often drizzly, afternoon out. There wasn't much ceremony. I don't think we ever had season tickets as a kid, we'd just make our minds up an hour or so before the match that we were going then we'd hop on the bus, whiz down Plungy and there we were, standing in the rain watching the Lilywhite's get covered in mud!

I moved to NYC in 2001 and the real football heads there knew of North End because of the famous US players that have played for the club: Eddie Lewis, Brian McBride and Eddie Johnson. Now I live with my family in a pretty rural town in Connecticut.

I coach the girls' football teams and occasionally you'll get a dad who's heard of PNE. Although oddly, when I was in the middle of nowhere in Colorado one year, I met a guy in some remote bar who knew North End really really well. He was a former Mormon and did his mission year in Chorley in 1996 and knew everything about Andy Saville!

Grandad was pretty sick before the end, but he spent his final days in a wonderful nursing home. We managed to get back and visit him before he passed away.

He got to meet my American Wife, and he'd regale her with tales of me as a ginger floppy-haired kid playing football for the cub scouts, and he'd be sure to tell her I was a bit crap!

Elsie Finney was at the same nursing home and Tom would visit her every day. Imagine that, an England legend just bimbling down the corridor every day. He'd stop in most rooms to say hi to the residents, little doff of the cap, a wave of his walking stick. He'd chat to my Grandad a bit too and it really made his day. And it's moments like these, these little interactions, which represent who this club is to me and my family.

To my Grandad, seeing Tom Finney walk by was nice, but it wasn't really all that unusual. This national hero was just a part of the community, and it's a great metaphor for our club. North End is tightly woven into the community of Preston and has been for over a hundred years. Our club has humility, a sense of community.

I'm at the point now where I've lived away from Preston longer than I was there, and the club now represents more than a team to me. It's a link to my childhood and my late Mother's side of my family. I definitely look through rose-coloured specs when I think of Preston, tho' the reality is probably a bit greyer. But when I'm 3,000 miles away, Preston North End is whatever I want it to be, I suppose.

'It's my true North.'

It's not fancy or precious, it's local, it's a shared experience, it keeps me humble, and it gives me hope.

Photo courtesy of Neil Jamieson.

RONNY VAN AUDEKERKE

ZELZATE, BELGIUM

I attended a lot of league games in the UK from 1992 onwards but never found a team that was right for me. Then a Belgian friend of mine – who is actually a fan of a posh London team – took me over for a game at Deepdale after he'd met a PNE fan on holiday.

It was against Burnley in 2011 when Phil Brown was manager. We lost 2-1 but the result didn't matter.

'The moment I entered the ground I was sold. This team in white was the team for me!'

I now try to watch PNE live four or five times a season, home or away. I fly with Ryanair to Manchester and then take the train to Preston. I go on the Friday and come back on the Sunday. If I'm over for a home game, I usually start my Saturday in one of the pubs on Meadow Street and after the game, go the same way back.

I have always been made very welcome by PNE fans whenever I've visited. At first, they were surprised to see a Belgian lad following their team because it's easier and more common for a foreign football fan to support one of the big Premier League teams. Even most of the Belgian football fans I know find it strange that someone supports a team like PNE.

Over here, most of them are members of organised fan clubs for the bigger English clubs like Chelsea, Spurs and Liverpool, or for the big teams in Germany like Dortmund, Schake and Bayern Munich.

This season, I flew over for the home games against Bristol City and Wigan, and also for the away game at Barnsley. But the Barnsley match was moved to a different date because of FA Cup fixtures that weekend so I ended up going to see Chorley v Halifax Town with some PNE mates because I'd already booked the flight.

Before the global pandemic, I had planned to visit for the Huddersfield Town match, not only for the game but also for a good friend's 60th birthday.

One time, when North End played Fulham away, I was invited for the first ferry crossing to Fulham by the London Branch of PNE fans so I took a flight on the Saturday morning from Brussels to Heathrow, but I could only watch the first thirty minutes because I had to be back in time to catch my return flight home, but it was all worth it!

About eight years ago, three PNE lads actually came over to Belgium and watched my home team, Beerschot, play. Then last season they travelled back over for a stag do with twenty+ lads. Again, they picked a game to watch and brought some PNE flags with them. It was great to see and everybody here still talks about it!

Supporting Preston North End and following English football is not only about watching ninety minutes of action. It's also about a good day out with some very good friends, getting dressed up and having a beer and a laugh. You know what time you'll meet up and start your day, but you never know what the journey will bring and when it will end.

Photos courtesy of Ronny Van Audekerke.

SEÁN CARR

CORK, IRELAND

My Mum is from Eccleston and I was born near the ground at Sharoe Green Hospital. Although I grew up in Ireland, I had frequent visits to see my Grandparents and Cousins which usually involved a trip to Deepdale.

In fact, my first memory of PNE is probably my Grandfather giving out about their results!

The first time I was at Deepdale was when my Dad and I visited the club shop to buy tickets for the game against West Ham on Saturday 23rd August, 1980. While we were there, my Dad saw that the ground was open and decided to have a gander around, and I remember the groundskeeper being delighted with my Dad's comments on the fantastic state of the pitch whilst kindly asking us to step off as there was a game on Saturday.

The first match I saw at Deepdale was actually a few days before that West Ham match, and was a reserve team fixture versus Everton. I still have the team sheet from the match which ended 3-3 after we'd led 3-0!

'In 2000, I got the chance to represent PNE as a journalist.'

I knew the club's Media Officer, Ben Rhodes – now the General Manager – and he got in touch with me, asking if I was going to any of the pre-season games in Northern Ireland. Due to work, I could only make one which was against Glentoran in Belfast. When I got to Glentoran's ground, I collected my Press Pass and set about reporting on the match. This was before up-to-the-minute commentaries, and I phoned in my reports from the Press Box to Ben at half-time and full-time.

Greegs managed to get sent off even though it was a friendly! And I met Moyise after the game and got a snap with him which was great. It was cool pretending to be a journo for the day. Everyone at Glentoran was so nice and I bumped into a few North End fans too. It was my first trip to the North since I'd lived there as a kid so, for me, it was a special event for many reasons.

Anyway, when I got home to Cork, I looked up a well-known PNE website and saw a few comments saying the match report was rubbish which I thought was hilarious!

The best PNE match I ever saw was the 4-0 win against Leyton Orient in 1995. I was there with my Dad and my Brother. Andy Saville's hat-trick sent us to the top of the 3rd Division that day!

It's a family tradition to support North End and I'm hoping to bring my young lad to Deepdale for the first time before too long. I once read that sport connects us to the adult world when we are kids. That's something I definitely felt growing up and especially to my Mum's side of the family. For me, PNE is the be all and end all!

Photos courtesy of Seán Carr.
Main photo (L to R) Seán and Oscar.

Sergio 'Conor' Tagliabue

GBS GIGLI BIANCHI, ITALIAN BRANCH

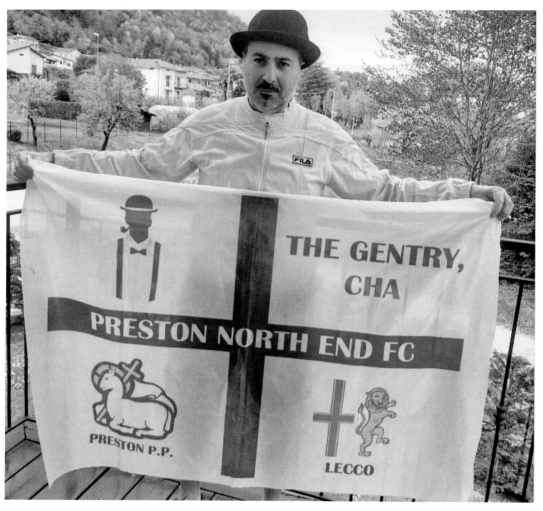

Being born in Italy, my passion for British football and PNE has been a gradual thing. I've always followed my local team, Lecco, but in the early 2000s, I grew tired of Italian football and started watching the Premier League on TV.

I was so impressed! The football was different to what I was used to. The cheering sounded beautiful, there were families at the stadiums, fans proudly wore their team's shirt and the stands were close to the pitch. I became fascinated and began reading books on the history of English Football, and then I came across a photo of the Invincibles. It captured my curiosity and I wanted to know more about this fantastic club called Preston North End who soon became *my* club.

The 23rd January 2010 was the first time I saw PNE play. It was on TV in an FA Cup tie against Chelsea at Deepdale. I remember that, despite PNE losing, I was fascinated by their stadium and fans. It was then I fell in love with the Lilywhites.

Following that game, I decided to open a blog where, to this day, I continue to write about PNE and provide match previews and reports. Later, I opened a Facebook page too through which other Italians got to know about my blog and from there, in 2010, we founded the first Italian branch of PNE and were officially recognised by the club!

The Italian Branch was born with great enthusiasm and has a dozen members from different areas of Italy. I commissioned an Italian graphic designer to create a logo of which every detail was decided by our members. In the early years, we produced a plaque which we awarded to Will Hayhurst as the best young player of the season, and also created two flags and a scarf. We presented one scarf to the club and placed another on the statue of Sir Tom Finney as a mark of respect.

In 2011, I attended my first ever match at Deepdale which was against Notts County. On that day, two former staff members, Gary and Adrian, were very kind to me and allowed me to tour the stadium and meet the manager, Phil Brown. Since then, my Wife, Silvia and I have visited the UK many times and I've been lucky to witness some great PNE games. My first Gentry Day – versus Brentford in London – is a special memory as I got to meet several PNE fans, and the cup match against Blackpool on the 5th August 2013 was an unforgettable experience!

Our GBS (Gigli Bianchi = Lilywhites Supporters) have now celebrated their 10th anniversary, and I hope one day to organise a meeting in Preston with PNE fans from all over the world so we can celebrate together.

I have experienced many emotions following PNE, but the most beautiful is having gained the respect and friendship of many English fans, and with this, I would like to dedicate a thought to Terry who has sadly left us.

Friendship with fellow fans has always been the most important thing for me. I am in all respects a PNE fan, despite being Italian, and I have also written a book about my support for PNE and the history of the club. Supporting this club has given me fantastic emotions, new and beautiful friendships, and it means everything. I dedicate a lot of time and passion to this club, and I do it with happiness and pride.

Photos courtesy of Sergio Tagliabue.

SIMEN A. PRAG
NORWEGIAN BRANCH

1930 - 2008   PNE FOREVER   40

ALLAN WILDING
1932 - 1985

LUKE MALACHI
KENYON 20.02.09

...DING
2009

OLIVER WILLIAM
KENYON 20.02.09

AND...
TRUE

JOHN UTTON
PNE YOUTH TEAM

CHRIS PARKER
FAN FOR 50 YEARS

DAVID MARSDEN
JANUARY 2010

PHIL PARKER
BEST GOALIE EVER

THE ON...
BOB TU...

...ND G HODGSON
PNE FOREVER

PAUL WALTON- PNE
IN ALL HIS PLANS

PETE MATTHEWS 09
PNE TILL I DIE

...URPHY
...ND ONLY

DEEPDALE
K R ROWE

EDWINA ACKLAM
BORN A LILYWHITE

PAT F...
NO...

NEIL, EMMA, NEMA
& EMIL DAWKINS

MICHAEL TARBUCK
NORTH ENDER

DAVID & BARBARA
***** HOGG *****

...DAM SHARPLES
PNE

BRIAN S... ...R
PNE

BENDIK, MATHS
& SIMEN PRAG

PETER
UP THE ...

& DAD
...REVER

SHEENA AND...
LOYA...

...E TILL I DIE
...IL MCDONALD

DAVE T KERRY
PNE 1955-1961

...THISTLETHWAITE
TOM'S NO.1 FAN

MELBOURNE
LOGAN PHILLIPS

DICK MAGUIRE
FOREVER WHITE

VERA HO...
90 YEARS ...

MATTHEW HARWOOD
30/01/2010

O'DONNELL FAMILY
BELCRUIT DONEGAL

Many years ago, long before the internet, Preston North End caught my eye when I was looking at the English League tables in a Norwegian newspaper. I took some time to find out about the club but it was a difficult task in Norway back then.

English football is big up north, but it was mostly top-flight teams who were covered at that time. Still, I kept my interest and, when the internet kicked in, it went from a keen interest to fascination. It was the badge, the name and the great history. Some choices are thought through, others are impulsive and irrational. Choosing to support PNE was a bit of both.

In 2009, I travelled over to see my first live game at Deepdale. I went with one of my Brothers and we fell in love with the club pretty fast after going through the gates. It was late fall, come early winter in Norway and it was very cold there, but we hadn't checked the weather report for Preston so we were the only people in the entire country wearing huge parkas to football that day!

Who are the Norwegian Branch? Well, I started to talk to Paul Whelan on Twitter and it kicked off from there. The group came together in 2009. First, me and one of my Brothers, then the third Brother came aboard and then two childhood friends of ours. We're not an official supporters club, we're just a few Norwegian lads that have gotten to know some English and share a love for beer, terrace culture and Preston North End!

Most of the lads live in or close to Oslo, except for me, I live a three to four-hour drive down south. We used to meet up for beers and watch Preston North End together a few years back but we live quite far apart now, but the lads in Oslo will meet up to watch the games on iFollow. We pretty much come over once or twice a year and have been to eighteen games in total, nine at home and nine away.

British football is and has been very popular in Norway my entire life. It's very common to support a team from England or Scotland. But not very many support Preston, so you get some raised eyebrows when asked who you support!

Over at your end, we've kindly been taken in and have had nothing but great experiences when visiting. Although we did nearly get our heads kicked in by a Wolves subway crew some years ago after a game in Wolverhampton, but our Scandi wits and charm got us through it okay!

We've never bothered the club itself for any attention and we've never tried to put focus on ourselves, but they have been very kind the few times we've interacted with them. They sent me a signed ball when my first child was born. I think Paul most probably had a hand at the wheel but it was a great gesture which my family really appreciated. Over the years, we've gotten to know people that work for the club and we are happy to call them mates.

Amongst our group, there's a mutual respect and love between us, just like in any group of proper lads. Preston is a family club and we're very proud and humble to be a part of that family. Since we began, there have been so many great moments big and small over the years and I look forward to taking my children, and the children of my Brothers and friends to Deepdale in the years to come.

Website: norwegianbranch.wordpress.com
Twitter: @NorwegianBranch

Photos courtesy of Simen A. Prag.

STU BENNETT

LOS ANGELES, USA

I used to bring the PNE players to wrestling shows whenever we wrestled in Liverpool or Manchester. The wrestlers really enjoyed meeting them and so some of them started looking out for North End's results.

I always tried to head over to Deepdale and Springfields for media work whenever WWE were wrestling nearby. Then one year, I was actually allowed to come and train with PNE at Springfields and Cody Rhodes told me he'd come along next time. Unfortunately, we were never able to arange it but Cody tells me he's a PNE guy now anyway.

There are a lot of footy fans in WWE. Most Brits there like the standard 'big' teams like Liverpool and Man United. The non-Brits who watch football are mainly the European wrestlers and the Mexican lads. They all seem to like Real Madrid, Barcelona and Juventus, but there's a Bulgarian wrestler called Rusev who follows his local team, Locomotiv Plovdiv.

Unfortunately, when I'm over in the UK these days I'm rarely in the North West as I'm mostly needed in London for work, or I'm in Cardiff where my parents and Brother now live. Whenever I manage to catch a PNE game live it's usually at places like QPR, Brentford and Walsall.

'Over the years I must've been to every lower division ground south of Birmingham to watch PNE play.'

I used to live in New York City and, last season, I met up to catch a game with a group of PNE supporters called the 'NYC North Enders'. They were a great bunch of guys and I wish I'd had more chance to hang with them. I'm now living in Los Angeles after two years in Manhattan. NYC is a great place but the hustle and bustle gets old after a while.

To keep up to date with North End I subscribe to the iFollow app so I barely miss a game but living on the West Coast means that the 3pm kick-offs are now going to be 7am kick-offs for me. I'm not a morning person so my coffee machine is going to be working overtime.

My Dad grew up a PNE fan and used to wait outside Deepdale as a kid so he could get Tom Finney's autograph. He would take me and my Brother to games. The first match he took me to was versus Mansfield Town in about '85 or '86. PNE were still on the plastic pitch but I don't remember too much about the game, aside from cheering for Oshor Williams!

As a kid, my heroes were almost always sporting, and I loved football. Aggressive players full of attitude have always been my favourite kind of player, players like Sean Gregan, Mick Norbury and Ben Pearson. I recently shot a film with Vinnie Jones and they're three enforcers who would make great villains in Hollywood!

A stand-out season for me is the 1999-2000 season. I was at university in Liverpool and was able to get the train over to a lot of PNE's home games that year. It happened to be the year we won Division Three and got promoted to what is now The Championship which, at that point, PNE had never been to in my lifetime. That team under David Moyes was brilliant and seemed to win every game 3-0. It was exciting and I loved the ride. I even got to see PNE away at Everton in the FA Cup, which was a great day out despite us losing 2-0. Twelve months later the same squad came within ninety minutes of the Premier League which was devastating and unfortunately lead to the breakdown of an iconic team.

Adapted from an interview in The Nosebag, Issue 2. Photo credit: The Nosebag.

STAFF

DENISE RATCLIFFE
RECEPTIONIST , 1993-2019

I'd never been to a match and knew nothing about football before I got the job of PNE receptionist. It was August 30th, 1993 when I started. Audrey Shaw, who was then secretary, rang me and said do you fancy working here on reception and ticket sales?

There were no computers, nothing like that. When we got to Wembley with John Beck in '94 we had to hand-write everyone's name and address on every ticket stub. It took us a month to hand-do these things because we were doing other work as well. That whole day of selling tickets we worked about eleven hours straight. Our hands were never right again after that! I remember Granada TV came to film the queue which went on for miles, and Paul McKenna's parents, who used to do the catering, brought a tea urn outside and were giving out tea to keep the fans going.

In those early days, my main job was answering the phones and enquiries at the window. That window was so low that we had to sort of bend down and look up to see the people on the other side. For selling season tickets we just had a red book, a pencil and a rubber. Fans would come and renew their seats and sometimes you'd get somebody saying, 'Oh, I've gotta move, I can't sit next to so-and-so this season. He drove me up the wall, never stopped whinging, thinks he knows it all!' Then you'd go on the stand with them and take the red book and say, 'What about this seat, this one's free?' and they'd say, 'No, I can't see with that stanchion.' And they'd be moving along, trying all the seats. 'Well this ones alright, who is in this seat? Oh, I'm not sitting next to them!' And so it would go on, but it was all about keeping the fans happy. I've got one of those wooden seats from the West Stand in the shed actually!

Going into the Pavilion, you entered the ivy-clad building through those old gates. You went up the stairs, there was the Ladies, the Ladies Lounge, then you went through a door and there were all the boxes. The Guild Lounge was up there too. Any visiting directors' wives or girlfriends went in the Ladies Lounge with our ladies. They could sit in the Directors' Box watching the match but they had to use their own lounge at half-time.

Ladies weren't allowed in the boardroom back then. There was a stained-glass window and the boardroom was all wood panelling. They had doilies and bone china teacups and the trophies on display. At the end of each season I used to have to take all those trophies home and clean and polish them. It was a bit nerve-wracking, especially the one with those owls on it. It used to wreck my hands!

I stayed as receptionist all the way through but of course the job changed over the years. I left in 2019 and my Daughter produced a book for me as retirement gift. I had a lovely time, got lots of kind messages, presents and cards, and got to parade with the players at the last game of the season. There is a great fondness there after 26 years. I met so many wonderful people and I like to think that people found me pleasant and helpful. A lot of the fans called me Mrs PNE which was really nice. They'd phone up and say, 'Is that the blonde lady with the glasses?' I had blonde hair then! I'll always follow PNE, they'll always be in my heart.

IAN ROBINSON
CLUB PHOTOGRAPHER

For me, a normal Saturday home match day starts about noon. First photos are usually of the dressing room and stadium followed by the players arriving, stadium tour, mascots, players' warm-up, players leaving the tunnel, match action and so on.

Selected images are sent from the back of the camera straight to the PNE media team. The last photos on match day are of the Man of the Match interviews and sponsors presentation, and I normally leave the ground about 6pm.

I don't really have a favourite photo. I usually have a favourite from each game but afterwards, you move on to the next match. I try and have a good relationship with the players and hopefully they'll remember to celebrate where I'm sat, but that's not easy in the emotion of the moment.

'You concentrate on getting goals, and I was very happy to get David Nugent's first goal after re-signing and also Scott Sinclair's first for the club.'

I used to work for the LEP and I was part of the photographic team who covered PNE home and away on a rota basis. My first game would have been around 1994 so I've been knocking around Deepdale for quite a while. After becoming freelance I was lucky enough to get work taking the match day mascots and corporate photos and now, this season, I've become the club photographer taking the match action for all games and fulfilling any photographic requirements the club needs.

For Sir Tom's funeral I was allowed on the steps of the church and not in the press pen, and when he was brought out of the church I was then on the top floor of the block of flats across the road. I think I was also the first photographer at Deepdale the day all the tributes started to be laid in his honour. It was a great privilege and an honour for me to be a part of it.

This job has given me so many memories over the years, like Deepdale Duck getting flattened in the players pile-on during the FA Cup game against Arsenal. Of course the 1999-2000 Division Two winning season is memorable, and the following season, getting to the Play-off Final in Cardiff, not forgetting Trevor Francis losing it on the touchline for the play-off leg at Deepdale. I can also remember listening to John McGrath's stories on an away trip to Walsall. I met John McGrath when he was a pundit; it was during the Brian Ellis days and we would occasionally take him with us to away games as we used to travel with the radio guys. John was a very funny guy with lots of stories and he kept us entertained.

Recently, I've seen some images I took for the LEP from the 95-96 season including Leyton Orient away and the last game of the season against Exeter at home. I'd forgotten what a great season that was! The old Town End was always full and bouncing and I remember ending up drinking in town with Gary Peters and Brian Ellis.

Some of the football that year was brilliant. At the time, you don't realise you're recording history. It was great seeing those images again and realising I took them. It really jogs the memory and shows how privileged you are to be involved, walking around the pitch as the team show off the trophy to the crowd. My only regret is I never had my photo taken doing it!

Photo courtesy of Ian Robinson.

JACK GORE
HALF-TIME PRIZE DRAW TICKET SELLER

My earliest North End memory is of going on with my family for a friendly against Leeds in 2001. My Brother had won the chance to be a mascot and, although I didn't get to meet any players, I did get the opportunity to do the stadium tour.

My Mum has always been a Preston supporter alongside my Uncle, but it wasn't until the 2003/2004 season, when my parents started collecting money for the lottery, that we became regulars. That was my first full season as a Preston fan, and up until about 2009 my parents got free season tickets for the family as a result of them collecting the lottery. After that, they were given the opportunity to sell the half-time prize draw tickets which allowed them free access to home games.

In 2011 I started selling the half-time prize draw tickets too. The job involves selling the tickets in the stands and then counting the cash before the game. The time we start depends on the kick-off time. On a Saturday, we usually start an hour and 45 minutes before the 3pm kick-off.

Most of the time, counting up the cash made from ticket sales runs over into the first five to ten minutes of the game which is just torture. It's always a rush to get the money counted, and I have missed goals on many occasions as I've been adding up in one of the rooms, but I love the job.

'One of the best parts, other than free entry to the games, are the relationships that I've built up with the regulars before the game.'

I always enjoy chatting with them about our recent form, upcoming games and updating them on the team sheet.

When it comes to my favourite memories, between 2005 and 2015 I was a part of the Young North Enders and was actually an away day mascot for ten consecutive years.

I really enjoyed meeting all the players each season over that time although, to be honest, I think Graham Alexander got sick of seeing me!

For best matches, the obvious option is Wembley 2015 when we smashed Swindon 4-0. Another is the first season that we got promoted. We had a home friendly against Hearts of Midlothian and the Scots brought down more fans from Edinburgh than any of the League One teams we'd played against the previous season. The atmosphere in the stands was absolutely electric!

Personally though, the memory that has probably stuck with me the most is being there for Graham Alexander's last game in 2012 and watching his last ever kick in football hit the back of the net. It was a game that didn't mean that much in the league, but the fact I was there when he scored his last goal is something that will stick with me forever.

JASINTA RYAN MAHAMBA
STEWARD

I remember when I was seventeen, I received a free PNE ticket from the landlord of the housing at Mill Bank Court. Ten tickets were given out to the children at the property and we all went to watch PNE play Stoke City.

It was August 1999 and PNE won 2-1. We were all very excited, not just to see North End win but also because we hadn't been to a stadium before and seen so many people in one place. I had no idea back then that I'd be working there one day.

I got the stewarding job on the Finney stand six years ago when I was pregnant with my last baby girl. I was on a security course and one of the NGTC staff told me to apply because PNE were looking for staff. I did an NVQ level 2 in Spectator Safety and First Aid and received my certificates, and I now work on the Bill Shankly Kop as a fire steward after gaining my fire training certificates.

One day, I was fire stewarding in the Sir Tom Finney stand, and had to check all the fire extinguishers and fire exits before the spectators came into the building. I also checked all the rooms in the stand including one particular room that said 'Directors' on the door. When I came out, a colleague of mine said, 'Did you just go into that room?' I said, 'Yes' and then, 'oh no, why?' He said, 'It's only for the directors and managers, no one else is allowed in!' I just gasped with worry thinking *Oh no, I'm gonna get told off now!*

'Working at PNE has made me more confident with speaking to different people because I was very shy.'

I'm quite confident now in a lot of things I do, especially when approaching spectators and letting them know if they are breaking any rules or regulations.

As a steward, I love meeting PNE fans on match day, especially those who have travelled from abroad to visit Deepdale and our city of Preston. I show fans to their seats if they aren't sure where to go and point out where they can get programmes and food and drink. I'm always on the watch checking everyone is following the rules on things like smoking, standing, having cans or even using racist language. I'm just there to help the spectators, and particularly so in the case of any emergencies.

As a steward, sometimes fans expect me to know everything about the teams and line-ups but all I can give them is basic information such as crowd estimates, match doctor, weather, match day passes, and whether it's a code green or a code black!

I hope to be working here for a long while because I just love the atmosphere and meeting and greeting people from all over the country. PNE is like my second home. I've made lots of friends and I really miss them when the season is over, but we all stay in contact by text during the summer. I know if I have any problems I can always count on the stand managers and other colleagues to help me out. We are a family at PNE and we all get on like a house on fire. I'm never off work unless I have an emergency. The spectators would know when I'm off because they can tell where their seats are as I'm always there on the same stand. I've been told if I'm not around they'll always ask the other stewards, 'Where is my friend, the smiley one?'

Photo courtesy of Jasinta Ryan Mahamba.

LEANNE NAYLOR
MSLO

MSLO stands for Match day Support Liaison Officer. It's a volunteer role and is something that's beginning to get drafted into every club. Hannah is our Supporters Liaison Officer. She's full time and is also the Disabled Supporters Liaison Officer.

This is mine and Janet's third year and Mark came on board this season. It was Hannah Woodburn, the Ticket Office manager, who got us into it. She was looking for sensible people she could trust, couldn't find anyone, and so asked me.

For a home match, we'll arrive at Finney's about 12:45pm, have a coffee and a chat, see what we've gotta do, which stands we should work on, decide if we'll work better as a group that day and so on. We go and see Hannah in the Ticket Office to get the match day notes and find out if there are any parties or schools on the pitch at half-time as we help out with all that. Then we'll have a walk around, have a chat with people, see if anyone needs help getting to their seats and make sure they know where they are.

'We know a lot of fans now and they always come over to speak which is really nice.'

We work up until kick-off and after that we're free to go and enjoy the game but we don't really switch off. If we see anyone that needs help, we are there to help. It's the same for away matches too and, especially with disabled supporters, our knowledge of the away grounds can be very important.

For away matches, I take Coach 1 at Deepdale, Janet has Coach 1 at Leyland, and Mark will take on 3 or 4. We arrange stewards for the coaches and run things like football cards during the journeys to raise money for different charities. Last season we raised £700 for Rainbow House alone.

When we're travelling on the coaches, we liaise a lot with PC Paul Elliott of PNE Police. Sometimes we can have thirteen or fourteen coaches on the road and he's great in letting us know if there's been an accident or any roads to avoid.

Paul is a great asset to the club, plus he joined us on the Big Sleep Out too. We've had many funny moments on the coaches and we always remember one about Ilene. It was Dress Up Day, or Grand National Day, and we were away at Bournemouth. There's a YouTube video, and Ilene had dressed up as a horse. She was there trying to warm up with the players and the stewards kept telling her she couldn't go on the pitch and she must stay at the side. Well, the next thing, she's off galloping across the pitch towards the players! It was hilarious. Most of our funny stories revolve around Ilene. She once even dressed up as a turkey at Burton on Boxing Day. We've missed her while she's been away. Coach 1 was renamed Ilene after the suggestion which was lovely.

My own favourite memory is of Wembley 2015. For the many weeks leading up to it, my life was chaos as we had 73 coaches to organise and my house was like a ticket office! But when I saw Wembley it was . . . Oh, the relief!

Paul's favourite memory is winning promotion when we played at Leyton Orient. David Beckham was actually stood behind him in the queue, and Janet's favourite memory is of meeting me! Oh, and the 6-4 Leeds match. Jon Parkin's hat-trick and all that. Happy days.

Photo (L to R): Janet McDonald, Mark Dickinson, Leanne Naylor.

LYNETTE WILLIAMS

FINNEY'S CAFE AND SPORTS BAR

On a regular three o'clock kick-off, we arrive early for a briefing before coming to Finney's Café. My position is that of Section Manager. On match days we usually have three agency staff: me plus two doormen.

I get to the café about 11:30am and start setting it up, getting it ready for when the agency staff arrive. I then go over everything with them and train them up if they're not sure about anything. We open the doors at 12:30pm and we're here until kick-off. After that, we'll clean up and get it all tidy, ready for Heartbeat. Then we're allocated to one of the bars on the stands. I'm usually on the Alan Kelly Town End but sometimes get placed on the Sir Tom Finney.

Doing this job has turned me into a North End fan. The first time I came to Deepdale was for Sir Tom Finney's funeral. I brought my Dad who was a massive PNE fan. When my Dad passed away, we scattered his ashes on the Finney Stand then just two months later I got this job and was allocated to the Finney Bar, so I feel it was meant to be.

In this job, I get to chat with quite a few PNE fans and they're all absolutely fantastic. We get our regulars coming in too. We know what they want now, so if we see them in the queue we can start getting their order ready. If you're organised, you can have a laugh with the fans. Many of them know me now and we have the craic with them.

A few weeks ago we had about thirty Danish PNE fans come in. They'd come over just for the game, big North End fans, and they drunk a lot of John Smith's.

This job means everything to me. It's my baby. I love it. As much as it tires me, I'd come here for no money. Since I've started working here, I've learnt a lot about football. I've even developed a tradition with a steward on the Finney stand which is, whenever PNE score we have to have a hug.

'I'm certainly a fan now, in honour of my Dad, really. I'm trying to get my Grandson into PNE as well, and he will. He will support PNE. I'll make sure of it!'

But this job can have its dangers. When North End played Middlesbrough in the Carabao Cup a few seasons ago, Callum Robinson knocked me out with a penalty!

I'd finished my shift on the concourse and the game had gone to penalties so I was going up to the away stand to watch the penalties and, as I was on my way, Callum stepped up to shoot, missed the nets and hit me on the side of head. I bounced me head off the wall and a steward caught hold of me. It was very embarrassing.

When I returned back to work, they presented me with the ball, fully signed, and it still had my lipstick on it! Of course, Callum did apologise and the ball now has pride of place in my bedroom. It was worth the concussion!

MATTHEW FLETCHER
MANAGER, PNE CLUB SHOP

Our busiest time is always kit launch. We plan ahead with the warehouse to see when the kit is due to arrive to make sure we've enough time to check it, count it into stock and then price and hang it up ready to go out on the shop floor.

Then there'll be pre-orders to send out as well. We try to make sure they arrive with supporters on launch day so they need to be picked, printed if required, and sent out a couple of days beforehand.

Over the years, we've had a few printing requests that we've had to politely refuse for various reasons! A few supporters always have the same name and number printed each season so we always look out for them around kit launch.

Most fans, especially the kids, tend to just want a player's name. There was a period when the clear majority of those were Joe Garner, but over the last few years it's been more even across the squad and I can remember doing at least one shirt for the majority of the first team squad this season.

Christmas is obviously another period when it's guaranteed to be busy, especially with internet sales and getting those orders out in time for the big day. We always send a lot of orders to fans in Australia too, so there does seem to be a decent PNE following out there.

We get a few players that come in regularly to buy items for friends or family. One day, a player came in and picked up a few shirts and other things. When he got to the till we asked if we could print the shirts for him and was it to be his name and number? The reply came back, 'No, my Nephew doesn't want my name, he wants *and he gave a name* as that's his favourite player.' It was the sense of disappointment on his face and the way he said it, we just couldn't help but laugh.

We also get our regulars who come in which is great. People pop in just to say hello or come in to talk about the latest transfer rumours. In fact, there's a couple in here that often I tell them I'm going to have to start charging them rent. They're in more than some of the staff!

'But that's the best thing for me, that interaction with the customers.'

I'm a Southend fan so I have my own burdens to bear, but some of the conversations I have with our customers I could be having with Southend fans, just with different names. It goes to show how similar football fans are. You are talking to other fans about a sport you love despite the ups and downs it puts you through.

When customers come in to buy items for funerals of supporters that have sadly passed away, their stories can be really poignant. And then the stories we hear from the older fans that come in, especially the ones that remember seeing Tom Finney play, can be really amazing. It's a privilege to hear them.

In total, we have three full-time staff and eight part-time who mostly work on match days. Some are PNE fans so they're working at the club they support. I've been here for seven years and my most memorable time has to be the play-off final in 2015. It was certainly one of the busiest two weeks I've seen in the shop but the general buzz around the club, and then actually going on and winning so convincingly, it was just fantastic.

https://pne.clubstore.co.uk/

NEIL HIGGINS
PROGRAMME SELLER

Sometimes it can be pleasantly warm, like early season in August, and sometimes it can be bitterly cold, but I put a bob hat on and all the rest of it, and you might think you look a bit silly but I don't care, I've got passed it.

But when your hands get too cold it can be difficult counting the money, and it's not really something you can do with gloves on. Getting the money out of your pocket when you've got cold and wet hands, that's tricky. But yeah, it's what they call a labour of love.

My Nephew started selling the programmes when he'd just left school but then he got taken on as a goalkeeper at Macclesfield Town so obviously he couldn't make Saturdays. He asked me if I'd do it occasionally and I ended up being full time. I've been doing this for over twenty years now and I shudder to think how many programmes I've got as I get one for free. I've a load of old ones in the attic. If I had time to look, it would be quite interesting.

I get here for about 12:45pm and go and pick the programmes up. Generally, on a big game, you can have anything from 300–500 programmes to sell. I get to my pitch for about 1pm and start from there. It gets really busy after 2pm and then I'll start packing up and wander back to the office two to-three minutes before kick-off.

We count up and check how many we've sold and, on a good day, I'll only miss the first five minutes and when that's done, you get on for nothing on the Town End, so it's good. Sometimes it takes longer and yeah, you miss the odd goal, but it's not too bad, and you always know if there's been a goal!

I'll sometimes see fans out and about and they'll say, 'Don't I know you from somewhere?' I have a lot of regulars. One guy who used to be a Special Constable arrives just after 1pm and always stays for about half an hour chatting.

Whenever I hear a foreign accent I always ask where they're from. A lot of Norwegians come over and I see some Irish and a few Scottish fans, so we are getting different nationalities and I find it interesting to meet these people.

Whenever I see anyone who isn't local, I always direct them to the Finney statue. I think that's a good thing for them to see. To be honest, I treat it like I'm an ambassador for the club even though I'm employed by a different company.

'I have a lot of banter with away fans too. I rarely see any trouble.'

I try to be polite and sociable. You're there in a big hi-vis, representing North End, so why wouldn't you try and portray a good image?

I've been going on since I was very young. Our next-door neighbours, who were season ticket holders, took me and my Brother on in the early 70s. I can vaguely remember the night match against Rotherham in '71 when we won the old Third Division. Ricky Heppelotte springs to mind and I certainly remember Alan Kelly Senior. I was on the time he went off injured and came back on again. And of course, there's Wembley. That's a great memory nobody can take away. Yeah, there's been a lot of happiness and good times. I feel a sense of belonging to the club, especially with working here, and I hope to continue doing this for a few more years.

PAUL BRADLEY
STADIUM AND FACILITIES MANAGER

My first game was the 14th November 1970 versus Rochdale. I went on the old Paddock with my Dad and older Brother. Dad called it pneumonia corner because there was no roof so the rain got you and the wind got you, but it was cheaper than anywhere else.

I brought my football and kicked it around the terraces. It was a cold horrible day but I didn't notice any of that. It's a bit vague but I can remember the goals going in and a penalty. I liked the drama of it all, the passion, the lights and the crowd, and we won 3-1! We gained promotion that year too so yeah, it really grabbed me.

It's a dream to work in this iconic stadium. I have 26 staff including cleaners, skilled joiners, plumbers and electricians. Some of them are big PNE fans too and I think it always means that little bit more when we've won and everything has gone right.

Two days before a game, we do a pre-match check on the fire extinguishers, lights, doors, heating and toilets. First and foremost, our fans must be safe. We have a pre-match meeting and are asked about any problems such as issues segregating fans, broken seats, how many floodlights are working and so on.

On a typical Saturday, we're in at 8am, sometimes earlier if television is involved. We try to have everything tested and ready for midday except for the lights which we put on at the referee's discretion. The ref might say I want them on for 2pm or 2:30pm but on a sunny day, if he doesn't request them, we try not to put them on because some-body has to pay for the electric.

It can be 8pm when we leave at night so it's a long busy day. We also work closely with Mark Farnworth, the Ground Safety Officer, who leads the team of stewards and is without doubt one of the best professionals I have ever worked with, and he's another big North End fan.

I've been here over nineteen years and have many memories but probably my most memorable, for all the wrong reasons, is the Leeds play-off semi in 2006. It's live on Sky and, suddenly just before half-time, the lights go out. Pandemonium!

'My boss rings me. Sky rings. The Ground Safety Officer rings, and all my friends are ringing asking if I want 50p for the meter.'

They're all comedians.

It's absolute chaos. The electrician at the time – who isn't the one we have now, I must add – says all the power has gone off, that there's a power cut in the area, so I radio through to the bosses saying the electrician thinks it's a power outage in the Deepdale area. Then I look across the road at the houses and through her window I can see little Elsie watching Coronation Street. I think, *oh bleep, it's us!* And it was. There was a problem with our main supply. Thankfully, we got it back up and running but it was a terrifying time, especially with the game being live on Sky. Let's just say the adrenaline was flowing!

I love this place and the people. Right now, this is the best it has ever been for me off the pitch and on it. I just feel we are really well run. We have a great maintenance team and a great set up right throughout the club. It's a fantastic place to be and I'm really proud to be here.

PC PAUL ELLIOTT

DEDICATED FOOTBALL OFFICER

When I first got the job I was called a Football Intelligence Officer. My main role was to gather intelligence and liaise with the other forces and clubs involved in fixtures to plan the policing response. However, with the rise of social media, the emphasis for me has changed.

The role has morphed into one of liaison and engagement – being an approachable contact point for all fans.

With the @PNEPolice page, I only agreed to do it if I could be myself and engage with people. A lot of corporate accounts are, well, too corporate. The whole point of social media is to be social; it's a conversation. It's important to treat people as adults. People know if they misbehave or cause trouble, they'll get arrested, they know that, so I try not to patronise.

I was very proud when PNE won 'Away Day of the Year' at the FSA Awards. The club were recognised by away fans and part of that is because the way we police is different at North End. We pride ourselves on it.

'We tell away fans where the best pubs are, how far the ground is, where to get a bus or a taxi. We welcome fans to Preston. It works.'

We get loads of praise. If we can be genuine with the fans, we reap the benefits later. If we have to deal with someone, the other fans can see that we've been fair and friendly all day and this person must've done something to warrant our response. It's a two-way thing; it builds legitimacy. A much better approach than being restrictive and confrontational. Over-the-top policing is counterproductive.

It's the same for the travelling PNE fans. I do my best to let them know of any travel issues and which pubs welcome away day fans. Where possible, I like to travel on the train with the fans. It's a great opportunity to build a rapport, have a laugh and see if they have any problems or issues we can help with. Of course, some don't want to be bothered by us and that's fine, I get that. Like at Fulham, I didn't go on the ferry. I was asked to, but they might have made me walk the plank. I preferred to wave them off.

But seriously, for things like that, you want people to just enjoy themselves and relax and sometimes the presence of Police can change the behaviour of people.

Policing football correctly is a big ship to turn around. I believe the best way to prevent disorder is to fully inform people and engage with them. Our principles are always the same: open honest engagement, welcoming, not oppressive, to guide and build that legitimacy. Football is a bit niche. In order to understand this job you must understand football's tribalism and subcultures. I'm an Everton fan, everyone knows that, so I understand what fans go through.

I feel lucky and privileged to have this job. I've built great relations with PNE fans and I want the team to do well, for them and the people at the club. I feel connected. In my head I'm not PNE's Dedicated Football Officer, I'm its Community Officer. PNE is a community. It's a family, and I'm part of that. Come Saturday afternoon or Tuesday night, whether you live in Deepdale or Norway, like some North Enders do, you're a part of that community and it's important you have a point of contact if you need it, and I see myself as that.

Twitter: @PNEPolice

PETER ASHWORTH
HEAD GROUNDSMAN

One funny story, although not very funny at the time, was when Phil Brown requested we put some ball stop nets up at the training ground so the team could train in different areas of the pitch and balls wouldn't be flying into people's houses and the adjacent canal.

This involved a lot of manual labour, digging and setting sockets in concrete, but we finally got everything done and took great pleasure in telling the manger he would be able to use them the next day for training.

We got in early the following morning to set them up so everything would be ready when the manager arrived. Feeling proud of our achievement, we then carried on with our daily tasks until the nightmare began. Just as Phil Brown drove in, one of the ground staff was driving past the new ball stop nets on a tractor and hadn't realised the netting had caught on the machinery. He then proceeded to pull down two sections of netting and two six-meter-high poles, all with the manager looking on!

Mr Brown shot into his office and I quickly followed to explain even though he'd seen it all happen. Luckily, I managed to tell him we could sort it before training and he took it quite well, although he did take great pleasure in calling in the man on the tractor and letting him sweat for a good few minutes. We managed to sort out the damage and get the nets back up for training, albeit with two of the poles a couple of feet shorter than the others, and everyone had a good laugh about it in the end.

Touch wood, we haven't had any major horror stories with the pitch but the biggest headache was when a previous manager proceeded to train on the stadium pitch every day, sometimes twice a day, for around three weeks in January. We had to watch on in horror as the pitch quickly deteriorated, knowing there wasn't much we could do to help improve the pitch in the depths of winter.

The worst part of this is the fans and people watching at home on TV have no idea what has gone on and just see a badly worn pitch. In this scenario you just have to grin and bear it and pray for spring to come early! The only thing we can do as ground staff is keep working hard, carry out the correct maintenance procedures and, as the grass begins to recover, ensure we get it back to its usual high standards as soon as possible. Fortunately, the season after this hard winter we went on to win the League One Pitch of the Year, and the dark days of that winter were soon forgotten.

'I'm very proud to be in the position I'm in and I understand what it means to the fans parting with their hard-earned cash to support the team they live for.'

It's great when we get nice comments from fans on social media if we post any pictures, and it's also nice if we have any visiting coaching staff come over and compliment us.

One of my biggest memories from my youth is of going into a football stadium and seeing the pitch in pristine condition thinking as I walked up the stairs, *wow, I'd love to play on that!*

If my team and I can give that wow factor to both fans and players on a match day, hopefully with a win at the end of it, then we know everyone's going home happy.

STEVE COWELL

KIT MAN

I was born a stone's throw from Deepdale at Preston Royal Infirmary but my formative years were spent growing up in Hesketh Bank near Southport.

Sadly, a chain of events led to us selling our family business – growing tomatoes commercially – and moving to Penwortham. Both my Father and Grandfather had died within a week of each other and this led to me completely withdrawing into myself.

I think I was about eight at the time and, more out of desperation than anything else, I was taken along to watch PNE as I wasn't talking to anybody. What happened then was the men inside the stadium suddenly became the men in my life that I was missing. From that moment on, an unbreakable bond was struck that will be there till the day I die.

I first got invited to play for the Supporters team when Gary Peters was manager back in the 90s. He was also player manager of the Supporters team and would play and manage them in the morning then jump in his car back to Deepdale to manage the first team! It didn't affect the first team's progress as we won the old Third Division title under his stewardship and also the Supporters team won their nationwide tournament the same year.

Gary actually dropped himself in the quarters to put me into midfield after a group defeat to Blackpool and the rest, as they say, is history.

I managed the Supporters team myself for ten years from 2004 and had quite a bit of success along the way. I only left as manager to take up the Kit Man job, or I'd still be there today. I'd been helping the previous Kit Man on and off for quite a while before being offered the job.

For five years, I was co-commentator for BBC Radio Lancs for all PNE away games and arrived at the ground the same time as the kit man so I used to give him a lift. It was Simon Grayson who asked if I'd be interested in taking over when the kit man retired. I never really thought any more of it until one day the club rang to see if I was still interested. I thought, this won't come around again in my lifetime, so I said yes.

'Home match days are what you buzz off, what you work all week for.'

Being a massive PNE fan, being part of the match day scene is a special feeling, and after five years, it still feels the same as when I started. Match day for a Kit Man has its moments but it's the day when you can really enjoy your job.

All the preparation is mostly done during the week. Turning up Saturday morning is all about checking everything is sorted and in place for both players and staff. Then you move on to pre-match equipment; you make sure the ref has the match ball plus some personal stuff like towels and drinks and then you can relax for a bit. I usually seek out the opposition's kit man for a brew and a catch up. Checking my pitch-side bag is important. You can't be out there without all the players' spare gear or you'll feel the wrath of the manager. Making the substitution is another job too. You have to know your squad numbers inside out or you're in trouble.

With the match over – hopefully with a win – it's then a matter of collecting all the dirty gear and getting them in the wash, making sure the players' boots and extra requirements are ready to take back to the training ground before closing everything down and grabbing a much needed beer on the way home!

10

AWAY

DAYS

JOE 'SMITHY' SMITH

It's all through my Dad. PNE is the biggest thing between us. He took me on the Spion Kop from a young age and I saw how Deepdale used to be. You'd come up that grotty hill, heading towards the ground, and it would all just open up. As a kid you're just, wow! What is this?

The first game I remember was in 1993 against Shrewsbury at Deepdale. Mike Conroy got a hat trick and we won 6-1! Goals were going in all over the place. I was thinking, *I could get used to this!* But being North End, you soon learn it's not always gonna be that way. I love away days and, again, it's my Dad's fault.

He started taking me the season we won the Third Division in 1996. We went to places like Barnet, Chester and Scarborough, but the one that really stands out is Leyton Orient. Momentum was building that season and you could just feel promotion was going to happen. We stayed overnight and he was explaining all night what promotion would mean to North End.

The next day, we travelled on one of the old London buses up to the ground. The away end was full and when Andy Saville scored our first, it absolutely erupted! I was only seven, going on eight, and I'd never seen or felt anything like that, it was just insane!

Saville scored thirty that season. I think his first was a header and for his second – which I fondly remember – their goalkeeper mishit a clearance and Saville sent it back over his head. When the ball dropped in, the place went absolutely wild! A bloke next to me jumped up in the air and landed with his elbow on the top of my head. SMACK! I went, AWWW! Quick as a flash, he whipped out a fiver and said, 'Don't worry about it, son, there's your compensation.' He walked away and that was it. I don't know who the bloke is but I got a fiver out of it and we got promoted, so that was a really good day.

We all went on the pitch afterwards and Leyton Orient kindly opened up two gates so we could exit the ground easily. A group of our fans took that as a cue to go to an off-licence around the corner and then proceeded to spray our fans with beer as they left the ground; it was absolutely brilliant.

I've done over 134 grounds now, old and new, home and abroad. For PNE away games, there's usually a group of five or six of us and we all club together. We like to get an early train and make a good day of it. We meet other fans along the way too. Sometimes we'll start off with five, and by the time we get in the pub at 10 o'clock, there can be ten or more which is brilliant.

'The beauty about following North End is that you can build your own little football family. It's always good times shared and memories made.'

To go through every emotion with family and friends, sharing the same cause, all trying to roar your team to victory, and then you see the ball hit the back of the net . . . Yeah, it's an escape. It's just amazing! I've got to mention Paul Huntington too. The Cumbrian Cannavaro is my North End hero, and never lets his performances drop. So much love for the big man!

Picture: Front: Joe Smith. Back L to R: Sam Weeden, Jonny Bacchus, Rob Reid.

JOHN SMITH

My association with Preston North End began in my childhood, being taken up from my home behind Fulwood Barracks to watch the PNE A and B teams play at the Willow Farm training ground.

North End's 3-1 giant-killing win in the third round of the FA Cup against Nottingham Forest in January 1969 provided me with an early Deepdale memory at the age of six. It was around this time I became a season ticket holder and used to sit with my Gran on the wooden benches in the old West Stand. Over fifty years later, that Forest match still remains one of my favourite games in over 1,200 visits to my spiritual home.

Other Deepdale highlights are the play-off games under the floodlights against Torquay and Birmingham. These matches produced an unforgettable electric atmosphere. And of course, there's the cherished memory of the 'Back in August on a Monday night' win against the 'team from the place with the tower' some seven years ago.

In the mid-70s I started going on away trips on Mercers coaches with my neighbour, Michael and other friends from Longridge. Then after becoming friends with a group from Ribbleton, we began to hire our own transport as away days became even more of an adventure, particularly overnight trips to Torquay, Bournemouth and Plymouth. On such trips, our early morning bleary-eyed arrival would be followed by a football match on the sea-front before going to enjoy pre-match pints in the local pubs.

My favourite away trip is Orient in April 1987: the first time I'd seen a promotion while attending a game. The party began on Friday night and, after a visit to No Nos, we boarded the 3am train, arriving in the capital for 7.30am. At full-time I joined hundreds of ecstatic North Enders on the pitch. The ripping of my trousers around the nether regions after scaling the nine-foot perimeter fence was a small price to pay to take part in the celebrations. I then fell asleep on the midnight train home and awoke the next day with a hangover in the railway sidings of Liverpool Lime Street, but I was still happy. After years of suffering with my team being the butt of jokes in the local pubs, I finally had a moment to enjoy.

By some strange quirk of fate, the next time we were promoted was at the same stadium almost nine years to the day. Again, there was another pitch invasion, and if anybody saw David Moyes disappearing down the tunnel in just his jockstap, boots and shorts, it was because I'd acquired his yellow shorts after much difficulty trying to pull them over his boots. Someone else beat me to his shirt!

Supporting PNE has always been a big part of my life and, over the years, I've enjoyed pre-season trips to Somerset, Scotland, the Isle of Man, Austria and Ireland. These trips have given me the opportunity to spend time with my PNE family, many of whom read my Fans Panel column in the LEP which I've been writing for the last nine years.

I always try to give an honest opinion and add some humour, and in the main I've received positive feedback. Although one reader did write to the LEP expressing a dislike of my references to television shows and fictional characters in favour of more match analysis.

With the pandemic, I feel like part of my life has been taken away but hopefully I'll soon be back travelling to away matches on Clem's Party Bus with my Longridge mates or in the car of Rick 'The Kirkham Love Rocket', my mate from the old Mercers coach days.

JONNY RICHARDSON

LONDON BRANCH

My earliest specific memory is a testimonial for Ricky Thomson versus Everton in 1982 when I was seven. Bobby Charlton was playing that night which was exciting as I knew he was famous.

My first competitive game was the FA Cup win over Blackpool at Deepdale in December 1982. It was a lively affair and, from that moment on, I got the bug. The next round draw took place on the radio immediately afterwards and we drew Leeds away.

'Can we go, Dad?'
'No.'

My first away game was in 1984 at Plough Lane of all places, as I live round the corner now, and I loved it. By the early 90s, we started to exploit away trips by jazzing them up, staying over in random places or taking major detours just because we could. It all began with Plymouth away in 1993 when my mate, Paul and I spontaneously took our passports and a significant detour by boarding the ovenight ferry from Portsmouth to Le Havre on a Thursday night. We sailed back from France on the Friday night, arriving exhausted at Plymouth to see PNE lose 4-0 on the Saturday. But despite the defeat, we were buzzing at what we'd achieved, and PNE Ferries, as a concept, was born.

More recently, the 'London Branch' flew out to Holland so we could sail back from Rotterdam to Hull for our game on the Saturday. We always discussed the dream of watching PNE in Europe, but as it's unlikely to happen in the near future, we thought such trips are the next best thing.

Sailing really is the best way to arrive at a destination, and we discussed doing something similar closer to home. Using the Thames was the obvious choice and the location of Fulham's Craven Cottage to Putney Pier made that the game to target. And so PNE Ferries made its official debut on the Thames in 2017 as 240 joyous

North Enders sang, danced and pyro-ed their way to

Craven Cottage. That first trip sold out over a weekend and coincided with Gentry Day, so it was a great day all round.

I'd been in London permanently since 2002 and around 2006 we played Burnley on TV on a Friday night. Sick of being outnumbered in pubs for North End games and knowing there were one or two fans in my neck of the woods, I put a message up on PNE-Online inviting them to a pub in Balham for the match. Seven PNE fans turned up that evening so the one Burnley fan was well and truly outnumbered and, fortunately, they turned out to be a half decent bunch! We're all still mates now and attend as many games as possible together, including some via ferry. If we're on TV, we're likely to meet up in one of London's many great boozers, but we'd much rather go to the games than feed Sky.

One or two have left London but we've since been joined by others in the capital. The name 'London Branch' was coined by a Preston-based fan and is the unofficial title for our unofficial group, currently numbering about twelve. We all chipped in for a 'London Branch' flag and carefully put together a design that uses the London tube font, an important detail to note. It's seen a fair few grounds now including Feyenoord's on our way to the Hull match. Over the years, many fans have got married and a number of kids have been produced which means a whole new generation of 'Cockney Whites' are about to hit North End games up and down the country.

KIM RAMSHEAD

Deepdale is just a five-ten minute walk from my house.— You can even see part of the ground from my bedroom, so it was inevitable who I was going to support.

I got my first season ticket aged about eleven and, before then, I used to go on a few reserve games with my Mum and Grandad. My Grandad was one of the main culprits for getting me on to games. I blame him for it! He'd been a supporter all his life and he used to sneak on Deepdale when he was younger.

One of my earliest PNE memories is from when they won the Third Division in 1996. I can remember putting on my PNE jumper and going to the flag market to see the team with the trophy. I was only six and Grandad lifted me up on his shoulders so I could see. It was a really fun day out!

I have so many PNE-related memories of my Grandad. In 2002 we played Stoke City at home and after us being in front, Stoke equalised three or four minutes into injury time to make it 3-3. I thought that was it, and Grandad said we should go because it was over, but we'd barely got out of our seats before Richard Cresswell popped up to make it 4-3.

I used to love listening to him telling me stories about games from the past, the good times at Deepdale and Tom Finney. Before my Grandad sadly passed away in 2014, going on the match used to be our little trip out and we'd always have some banter and a laugh. Once, at Deepdale, we wore our bowler hats with pride and so now, every Gentry Day, I get to remember him that bit more.

In 2013, the PNE Player of the Year awards ceremony was held on my birthday. Halfway through the evening, the lights were turned off and the host began talking about it being someone's birthday. I heard my name and then Bailey Wright walked towards me carrying a birthday cake and card! Everyone in the room started singing happy birthday to me.

'Not many people can say the whole PNE squad have sung happy birthday to them.'

It's a night I'll treasure forever, and let's just say the drinks were free for the rest of the evening.

I love away games and, in the past twelve years, I've only missed two. I go on the official coach from Deepdale, now named 'ILENE'. The journeys to and from the games are brilliant. There's a small group of us that sit at the front of the coach, and every trip we have a laugh and talk about what we thought of the game and so on. And we've had some adventures.

In 2009 or 2010 – I forget the date – our coach broke down just ten minutes after leaving Cardiff's ground but we managed to keep cheery and warm with plenty of brews at a local service station thanks to a Welsh coach company who got us off the motorway.

My favourite away game is obviously Wembley but there's also the 6-4 win at Leeds and Jon Parkin's hat-trick. Now, that coach journey home was very cheerful to say the least!

I took my Goddaughter to her first game recently. Seeing her face light up going into the ground made my day and to top it off, we won! I have met many people through following North End and some of these I can call my close friends. For me, supporting PNE is one of the best things to do.

MIKE FAULKNER
FLAT CAP DAY

Flat Cap Day was the last game of the season away at Bolton on the 8th May 1993. I think we were already relegated by then. I was at Runshaw College, a bit older than seventeen.

Me mate had just learnt to drive so we travelled down in his Renault 5 to Bolton, to the old Burnden Park with the supermarket.

One mate had his face painted in blue and yellow stripes, another had a flat cap whilst I, I don't know why, had this silly yellow wig on. The away end was full. The atmosphere was brilliant and it seemed everybody had a hat on apart from me. There were lots of songs but all I can remember is the old Hovis tune. They were handing out the song sheets on the day. It was a bit unusual to have a song sheet and stick to it, but it was well orchestrated.

In the match, John McGinlay scored a penalty, we got relegated and they went up. At the end, their fans invaded the pitch and started coming towards us. I thought, *oh no there's going to be a load of trouble*, but there wasn't. They came over and just applauded us and we clapped them back. It was a sign of mutual respect, a nice touch to be fair.

The song sheet is still in quite good condition. They used to do a fanzine as well called Pie Muncher and my Uncle used to buy it all the time. He was about 24 and I was ten years younger. He'd be laughing his head off then I'd read it but wouldn't really get it!

I've had so many laughs with my mates going on Deepdale and travelling away. I used to go on the coach as a kid and can remember Whitley Bay. I was still at school and we went on a Fishwick bus. We were speeding down this hill and the bus was going through the gears and I was thinking, *we're going a bit fast here*. We were literally flying down to the coast on this Fishwick bus. Anyway, the driver eventually pulled over, turned round and said, 'Me brakes aren't working!' It was quite a scary experience, and we got beat 2-0. The worst day ever.

My Great Uncle took me to my first PNE game in the 1985/86 season. I didn't go to many games but I got the bug and the next year he got me a season ticket. It was the promotion season under John McGrath. He was a brilliant manager and had such charisma. It was a great time to watch North End, and my first ever shirt was the Garratt's one they had that season.

We used to sit in the West Stand above the Crazy Corner. When I got to about thirteen or fourteen, I looked down and saw a couple of me mates in there so I used to go down the stand and speak to the steward and he'd let me in and I'd be there jumping about with all me mates. Then I'd go back to me Uncle just before full-time. When I reached fifteen or sixteen, I started going on by meself with my best mate, Neil Reynolds and we became permanent fixtures in the Crazy Corner. It was a really small section and, when I look back, there were probably around 200 of us in there but at the time it felt like 10,000! You know, as a kid it's just an unbelievable experience. Good, happy memories.

MIKE 'MICK' SMITH

Living in Deepdale on Burrow Road and attending Deepdale Primary School, I was always aware of PNE and, although my Dad and siblings were not interested in football, I always looked for the PNE result on Saturdays.

I didn't start going on until after the 1964 FA Cup Final, but that cup run really sparked my enthusiasm and I remember going to the Flag Market in front of the Harris Museum to welcome the team back from Wembley. From that day on, I was hooked and would go on Deepdale whenever I had enough spending money to afford it.

I saw a lot of games the following season but, unfortunately for me, I missed the last home game which was the 9-0 thrashing of Cardiff. At that time, a light aircraft used to circle the town trailing a banner with the current score. The pilot must have come close to running out of fuel that day! The next season, I'd saved up enough money to buy a season ticket for the Spion Kop, so I was always there ready for another 9-0 thrashing.

During the 1975/76 season, a group of regular PNE away day supporters decided to raise money to help our beloved club out of financial difficulties. After some debate, the consensus was a sponsored walk was the best option, and with an away trip to Bury on the horizon it was decided that was the perfect challenge. And so, in the early hours of Saturday the 21st February 1976, fifteen hardy, loyal supporters set off for Gigg Lane at various times.

Along with four or five others, I decided to set off at 1am to ensure we arrived in time for a couple of pints before kick-off. I can confirm no prior training took place and we set off without a planned route, but after trudging thirty miles in awful weather we arrived at the ground, by some miracle, around 1:30pm which gave us ample time for some welcome refreshments. We were knackered and soaking wet but it didn't matter!

Overall we raised around £300, which was a fair amount back then. To thank all fifteen participants, the club invited us as special guests to the next home match which was against Chester City. That was the one and only time I sat in the old Pavilion Stand, but sorry to say the match was a drab, goalless draw.

Over the years, I've had many favourite players and Alan Spavin, for one, is a player I feel was often underrated. Then as a strike partnership I thought Bruce and Elwiss were superb. My favourite PNE manager has to be Alan Ball Senior. He brought passion back to the club when all seemed doom and gloom and was the man responsible for the gentrification of PNE.

'My Wife, Sheila always used to say to me I had three loves in my life: Preston North End, Boddingtons bitter and herself, and she was never sure where she ranked!'

These days, true Boddingtons is no longer available and I now have two great Sons, Daniel and Kieron. So if Sheila reads this book she can know that she comes first, then the boys and then North End . . . honest!

PAUL WHELAN

I've got the champagne bottle that David Moyes sprayed the crowd with away at Cambridge in 2000. It was bank holiday, Easter Monday 24th April. We'd just lost 2-0 to Cambridge United but other results meant we'd won promotion.

Moysie came charging out with this bottle of champagne and started spraying it into the crowd. I just grabbed it off him, took a swig and then handed it back, but he didn't want it so we had half a bottle of champagne on the way home.

When we got back, we went into Squires and had the night of our lives. We were students and Monday night was Students' Night. We were in the VIP area for some reason, I don't know why, but one of the bouncers came over and said, 'You'll have to move lads, the North End players are coming into this area now.' I said, 'I'm not moving, I come here every week.' and he said, 'Yeah, you do actually. You can stay.' So we stayed in the VIP area and all the players came in.

There were about five of us and the whole team. It was surreal. The whole place was buzzing. It was a bank holiday, it was Easter AND we'd just won promotion. Then the players started swapping their North End shirts and t-shirts with people for anything at all. It was bizarre.

I got Michael Appleton's and Ryan Kidd's training jackets and my friend swapped his brand new Lacoste polo shirt for Jonny Macken's top, his sweaty Lacoste polo shirt that he'd been wearing all day! I remember Tepi Moilanen coming out half naked because everyone was taking his clothes off him. He just had his house key around his neck so that he didn't lose it. And then David Eyres dropped his phone and it smashed everywhere and my Brother picked it up and fixed it for him. It was just a silly old night.

We went to Stoke last year but there's nowhere to drink at Stoke. You come off the station, there's a hotel opposite, a pub about half a mile down the road and that's it, but there is a bar in the station so we walked in there.

There were probably fifteen to twenty of us and the doorman stopped us and said, 'Sorry, no football fans today.' My brother turns up, who is about 6ft 3in, a cancer nurse and a real gent, but he looks hard as nails, and he said, 'No, we're just here for a train convention.' and the doorman said, 'Ah, well you can come in then, lads.' We didn't look anything like train spotters. We didn't have our notebooks anyway! But yeah, I just like finding a pub and talking to people in the bar and seeing how their season is going. I think I've done about 86 out of the current 92 grounds now. I prefer the old fashioned grounds, places like QPR where you're quite close to the pitch.

When we were younger, a Great Uncle on my Mum's side lived on Lowthorpe Road next door to what was the club shop. When I was about four, my Mum used to take me round there after school and when they opened the gates twenty minutes early to let people out she'd take me on and let me run around. That's how I started, but my first real season was the 86-87 promotion one. A lot of the things I've done in my life have been PNE-related in some way and nearly all my friends I've got are through Preston North End. This may sound daft, but North End, it's my life, It really is.

'We've had some good times going away.'

Photo (L to R): Paul Whelan, Ian Bashall, Ian Small, Andrew Clement.

Photo courtesy of Paul Whelan.

TOGETHER

WE

ARE

INVINCIBLE

AISHA MUSA

ISLA HITCHEN

LUKE CARTER

JAMES POND

11

COMM-
UNITY

ADRIAN MURRELL
WINDRUSH INITIATIVES CIC

In 1886, Arthur Wharton joined Preston North End as an amateur to become the first Black footballer to play with a professional side.

It's a significant moment in the club's history and something they are rightly very proud of but, over a hundred years later, I didn't see many Black supporters of North End. This just didn't seem right to me, especially with Preston having the largest Black population around this district, more than Chorley, Leyland, Blackburn, Blackpool or Burnley.

I was thinking about this as racial abuse of Black players was in the news and I'd just seen the likes of Tammy Abraham, Marcus Rashford and Raheem Sterling all receive racial abuse within weeks of one another. As I sat there thinking about Arthur Wharton, I also recalled watching Man United v West Brom on TV in the 78/79 season.

Gerald Sinstadt was commentating and that was the first time I heard a commentator mention the booing of Black players. I remembered being shocked and angry and wanting West Brom to win, especially with them having 'The 3 Degrees' (as they were affectionately called) of Cyrille Regis, Laurie Cunningham and Brendon Batson. I'd never seen 3 Black players play in one team before and it filled me with joy but I also hoped they didn't make a mistake. So when Cunningham and Regis scored, I was so happy, especially with Regis being the spitting image of my big Brother, Malvern Dyer who was a season ticket holder at Deepdale and the man who first introduced me to the Lilywhites in 1968. Malvern sadly passed away in 2005 but his daughter and grandchildren carry on the tradition as PNE season ticket holders.

I'm the founder and CEO of Windrush Initiatives in Preston with many years of experience in community and youth work, and so forty years after that West Brom match and I'm still seeing Black players being booed, I just couldn't sit there shaking my head in disgust. I felt I had to act.

I sent an email to Tom Drake of Preston North End

Community & Education Trust and asked him for a meeting. I explained to Tom that we (Windrush Initiatives) felt as an organisation we had to do something and asked him what could we do to help PNE combat racism. Tom said that he thought they could do more and was prepared to see if we could work together to start encouraging more Black people to come and support a team they only supported from their armchairs.

I explained to Tom that we hadn't had a football team in Preston from the African/Caribbean community for more than two decades and it would be a great achievement if we could form one. Tom agreed and, with the help of North End, proceeded to help. Out of that meeting, Windrush United were formed. PNE Community & Education Trust sponsored their kit while ourselves at Windrush Initiatives sponsored the new Windrush Community Trophy. And so on the 22nd June 2019, a momentous occasion took place. 71 Years after the 'Empire Windrush' landed at Tilbury Docks, Essex, carrying 492 migrants from the Caribbean who had come to help rebuild post-war Britain, the great grandchildren of those passengers represented them in a fantastic football match in honour of that important landmark in modern British history.

I'm happy to say Windrush United won 9-1, but it wasn't about the result. It was a fantastic day all round and a match for the Windrush Community Trophy will now take place each year as Windrush Initiatives and PNE Community continue to work together to forge stronger and lasting links between the Black community and Preston North End.

Twitter: @windrushCIC
FB: @windrushinitiativesCIC

Trophy and team photos courtesy of Adrian Murrell.

JOE WALMSLEY

My course at UCLan – Sports Coaching and Performance – offers a module named International Development. If you take this module, at the end of the year you are given the opportunity to go to Kabawe in Zambia.

You get to help Sport in Action deliver sports lessons that teach about STDs and other vital information in Africa. Whilst there, you are also able to go to the community field and play with the children who aren't able to go to school.

Each member on the trip takes over a suitcase full of sports clothes to donate to Sport in Action who then hand them out to those most in need in the community. So, before I went to Zambia, I posted an appeal on the PNE Fans Forum page on Facebook to ask if anyone had any spare kits they'd like to donate. Through this, a member of staff from PNE contacted me and offered to donate some PNEFC kit from the club which was great! My fellow students then went to the training ground to collect the kit from some of the players.

The youth and adults in Kabawe loved wearing the PNE kits.

'A lot of the time, they will just wear clothes that are ripped and damaged so having brand new kits to wear, especially for their teams to play in, made them overjoyed!'

I think this trip has been going on now for over a decade, so the community will know a bit about PNE due to the students coming from Preston each year. However, I think this is the first time PNE have donated full squad kits, so maybe the club's following will now start to grow over there.

Since I've been back from the trip, everybody has been so excited to hear about it and how life is over there, and of course it's great to talk about.

It does sound very stereotypical, and I don't like to say it, but it was such an eye-opening experience. They only have around three footballs for over 200 kids in the community and they make their own footballs by balling up plastic bags and tying them together. It's great to just bring their story to light of how positive they are with so little.

Receiving support from the club for my trip was fantastic and PNE are one of the most important things in my life. I was born and bred in a PNE household and therefore have supported them from a really young age.

The first match I can remember is the Play-Off Final at the Millennium stadium against West Ham. That was probably my first season as a season ticket holder when I was aged around seven or eight. My Girlfriend will often joke that I love them more than I do her so I think that sums up how much the club means to me! I'm also currently doing an Analysis Work Experience within the PNE Academy which has just grown my love for the club and allowed me to help those coming through the ranks.

Link to Zambia highlights video:
https://youtu.be/wPRp5aDUtA8

Zambia photos courtesy of Joe Walmsley.

STEVE ELLIOTT
SPORTING MEMORIES NETWORK

My Dad took me along to a trial at Nottingham Forest. I was only sixteen at the time and afterwards quickly got out of the way, but Brian Clough came walking over and said, 'Would you like to play for me, son?' I said, 'Yeah, okay.' And that was it.

I just wanted to play football. I loved it. When I started out, Cloughie used to have us cleaning the First Team players' boots and sometimes he'd throw in his kids' school shoes too!

Nobby Stiles signed me for North End in 1979. As things went on, it was hard because the club was struggling for money but it was a fantastic move for me and my career and of course I met my Wife, Mags! We had some really good players in my time and the banter was great fun. I remember Brian Taylor, Eric Potts, Don O'Riordan, Sean Haslegrave, Andy Mac, Roy Tunks . . . I could go on and on. So many great names. Oh, and Alex Bruce. Brucey was a good one, wasn't he!

I still support PNE and go on the matches when I can, and I still play, turning out for the walking footballers every Thursday, which I love! Come Tuesday, I'm itching to go.

It's important for me to stay active. A year before my 60th, I was diagnosed with Alzheimer's/head trauma which has seen my life change dramatically. My Wife has been amazing and comes with me to all the Sporting Memories groups. Sporting Memories is structured to my week. It gives me a lot of pleasure meeting different people and interacting.

Alex Bruce – who is a volunteer – also comes along to the sessions. He's good, is Brucey. The sessions consist of quizzes and games, including football penalty shoot-outs, putting competitions and table tennis. People bring memorabilia, photos, programmes, old football boots, and it's not just footy stuff. They have a lot of guest speakers too from various walks of life.

All the people that go are a really nice bunch and I look forward to it. It really helps, and of course the games can get a bit competitive! It brings back a lot of memories and has the trigger factor for people. They all come back, so the group must be doing something good!

Steve made 208 appearances for PNE, scoring 70 goals. Sporting Memories Network: Using the rich history and heritage of sport, Sporting Memories clubs are open to any people over the age of 50 who enjoy reminiscing about their experiences of watching or playing sport. The clubs take place each week and are a friendly, welcoming environment that is open to all. Many members attend to enjoy the company of other older sports fans, some members live with dementia or have memory problems, some have experienced depression, they may have had a stroke or live with Parkinson's, all have one thing in common, a love for sport!

The clubs always have volunteers or staff present who have been trained by Sporting Memories to lead the sessions which use a wide range of Sporting Memories reminiscence resources developed specifically to help prompt conversation and discussion.

Sessions:
Players Lounge, PNE, Deepdale Stadium, Deepdale, Preston. Tuesdays, 11.00 – 12.30.
Lancashire FA, The County Ground, Thurston Road, Leyland, PR25 2LF. Mondays, 11:00 - 12:30.
Chorley Football Club, Victory Park, Duke Street, Chorley, PR7 3DU. Wednesdays, 13:30 - 15:00.

For more info visit: www.sportingmemoriesnetwork.com
@pnecommunity @SportsMemNet

TOM DRAKE

HEAD OF COMMUNITY, PNE COMMUNITY & EDUCATION TRUST

We engage with over 11,000 people a year and deliver 26 different programmes across the areas of sports participation, education, health and social inclusion. We cater to the needs of local people and help place PNE at the heart of the community.

We're here for the community and that's one of our challenges. We're a hidden gem. We do all these unbelievable programmes but does everyone know about them? Not yet, but hopefully they will do.

Earlier this year, through our PNE Forces programme, we signed the Armed Forces Covenant which is a pledge between the Club and the Trust, to continue to support past and present members of the military and their families. Every Wednesday, we run a football session for veterans; they turn up and participate and then represent PNE against other veteran initiatives. We also run a welfare support to help with housing and food. The impact of this project has been absolutely immense and we're really proud of it.

Something else we've done this year is to help with mental health. We've had a couple of young fans we've supported recently and they're now in a bespoke mental health programme that we run, and we're also launching a mens mental health programme which is going to encourage fans and the community to come forward as individuals and speak to each other. Currently, mental health is on the agenda everywhere so it's important we provide for the community.

We can't do everything, but we can do what we're good at, and that's being diverse and using sport and PNE as a tool to engage with people. Our education projects include working in nurseries, primary schools and high schools. We run our PNE Community Post-16 course programmes with young people doing BTEC level 2 and 3 with us, and also run a degree programme. For our disability programme, Every Player Counts – which provides opportunities for disabled adults and children to get involved in football – we've partnered with local charity, Sir Tom Finney Preston Soccer Centre, to provide free sessions every week. Our women and girls programme, along with adult programmes like Walking Football and our Sporting Memories group, continue to grow, and this range of activities ensures we impact the lives of all age groups.

The players at this club are absolutely fantastic and heavily invested. One example is Louis Moult with the Big Sleep Out campaign. Louis was willing to use his own story to encourage people to get involved, and you won't see many players stood on a cold concourse during an international break till 9 o'clock shaking everybody's hand. But that;s Louis and he sums up the players at this club. It's something that goes missing, but PNE as a club, and the players, are unbelievable.

The Sleep Out was a huge inspiration. We'd put months of planning into it and the taget we'd set between us, Foxton and the other partners, was £50,000. To see 300 fans and community packed into the concourse, well, I just thought it was unbelievable, and within a week after the event, we'd hit £90,000. There's just a real community feel here, that's what the PP in the badge is for. We've also seen a spike in our relationship with the forums who were a massive force behind the Big Sleep Out. We're trying to work better with them and it's important we do to promote our community arm.

We have a team who are so passionate and carry the badge with pride. Football is powerful, and PNE and the badge are extremely powerful. Combine them, and you can remove barriers and change people's lives.

Website: https://www.pnefc.net/pnecet/
Twitter: @pnecommunity
Photo credits: Ian Robinson/PNE Community

JUNIOR WHITES

MICHELLE HAYTHORNTHWAITE & JAMIE FOGG

Junior Whites provides a match day experience with football-related activities for young fans. It's all about taking it outside of what they see on the pitch and giving an insight to behind the scenes.

We do ground tours so kids get to see the environment and, over time, build up the overall football club picture. For instance, we can go and see the referee or go up to the media room and meet the reporters. We might sit by the media bench and listen to them doing the commentary and audio or visit the changing rooms and meet the players. It's all about making them think deeper, see the bigger picture. Plus, we make things and start projects they can take home – all revolving around a football theme.

If you think about the adult fans, many have their rituals where they go for a pie or a pint before the game – well this is a ritual for the kids. They'll come and eat here, meet friends, do the activities and then go see North End play.

Sometimes we get parents who aren't football fans, and this is a good way to absorb them into their kids' passion. The Junior Whites all sit together in the Sir Tom Finney Family Stand. It's quite community based and, as some parents may sit in another part of Deepdale that might not be so child friendly, it means everyone can still enjoy the game. Although we do have parents who collect their kids before kick-off because they want to watch the match with them. We are very flexible, and if parents just want their child to have the pre-game experience, or even arrive halfway through, that's fine.

Deepdale Duck is always here; he's brilliant and is part of the furniture, and the players visit too. They're such nice fellas and the kids have a great laugh with them. Sometimes the kids can be all cocky, like they can be, but then a player will walk in and it goes deadly quiet. They get starstruck! But the players are really relaxed so then the kids relax.

Once they've met a player you can hear the kids cheer that player on the pitch. It's lovely to see the connection, especially when they get the player's name on their shirt.

We're linked to the Soccer Schools as well and many players come to those. Gally, DJ, Darnell and Barky, they're all amazing and just muck in, but we'll never forget when Ben Pearson came and one of the kids tackled him and absolutely floored him. He absolutely floored Ben Pearson! They were a bunch of ten-year-olds and Ben was on the floor, but he was great about it.

'It's fantastic to see the impact they have on the kids.'

And they don't just do the soccer side, they've joined in a few tournaments on the Xbox as well.

You can be a Junior White from birth and you don't have to live in Preston or England to join. Membership is £30 for the season and members get an exclusive Junior Whites membership pack which includes a scarf you can't buy in the shops, a bag, gloves, poster, autograph book, newsletters and much more. The match day club is for ages 4-14 and runs from 12:30pm to 5pm. It costs £10 on the day, and that covers a match ticket, food, a drink and all the activities. Many parents are jealous of the activities as some things are just not ordinarily accessible to adult PNE fans! Junior Whites is fun and educational, and through it we hope the children will grow to become lifelong North Enders.

www.pnefc.net/pnecet/community-engagement/junior-whites/

TERRACE
TALK
2

12

KIERON RHYMES

The first time I went on Deepdale was around 2004 for a match against Gillingham when I got a free ticket off a mate at school. I didn't go again until after I'd left school when I went on with some mates, and I just really enjoyed it. And that was it. I was hooked!

I got a season ticket and started going on all the time. I remember that season well. The three new stands had been built but the old Pavilion was still standing.

I'm an amputee and play some football myself. In 2013, I hurt my left leg playing football. I have neurofibromatosis which led to complications with the injury and eventually I had to have my leg amputated from below the knee.

A while ago, I saw a post on Facebook on a group called Away Days.

'An amputee who was a Grimsby fan had posted a photo of his Grimsby shirt that said 'Peg Leg' on the back. I'd never thought about doing that.'

Then I saw one from a Colchester fan with one leg who'd got 'Legless' printed on his shirt. I thought I'd get one done for the fun of it and then I put a photo up on one of the forums. It got a great response from our fans when I posted it. Some praise and many laughs which was nice.

A few years ago, my friend, Shabir, nominated me for the Christmas PNE Shining Star. He put me forward because my Dad had undergone a triple heart bypass and my Daughter, Ellie, had endured brain surgery at just four years old. Shabir thought I'd been through a lot and deserved a treat. This resulted in four PNE players turning up on my doorstep – Scott Wiseman, Kyel Reid, Jermaine Beckford and Paul Huntington. Oh, and the Deepdale Duck, in plain clothes!

They brought me a hamper and stayed for about twenty minutes. I had no idea what was going on.

These days, I go on the games with my lad, Tyler, my mate, Shabir, and his son, Adam, and sometimes Ellie comes along too.

I go to quite a few away games. The 4-6 away at Leeds stands out for me. That was a good one that!

I love following North End. All my family are supporters and the club means everything to me. I just wished I'd started going on sooner.

Photo (L to R): Tyler and Kieron.
Insert photo courtesy of Kieron Rhymes.

LUCY CROMPTON

When I was younger, my Brother, Philip, and my Grandad used to go on together and when Philip got a little bit older I would go on. Now that I'm older, I take Grandad on but it did used to be the other way round.

It wasn't my first game but I remember travelling on the coach to Cardiff to play West Ham. My Brother and Mum went too and we had flags and a horn. I seem to remember they wouldn't let us in with the horn.

A while ago, I took a picture of my Grandad in his new PNE shirt that had 'Finney' printed on the back. I posted the pic on Twitter and it got over 200 likes. He wears it to every game but can't wear it next week as we're going in the Invincibles Lounge as a treat for his 80th and he has to wear a shirt in there. The feedback from the photo was great. He was a minor celebrity!

Grandad has a few North End stories. He remembers going to Liverpool when he was about nine and being in an enclosed area for young people where everybody was fenced in. North End won thanks to a Finney penalty and Billy Liddell missed one for Liverpool. That was probably around 1951 or something like that, just after the war.

In those days, when he went on North End, he'd walk down Moor Park Avenue amongst huge crowds of people. He says after the war it was full of American soldiers who lived in old Nissen huts that ran along the left hand side of the avenue. Grandad says they used to ask the soldiers 'Got any gum, chum?' and the soldiers would give them strips of chewing gum. The soldiers were waiting to go home after the war and when they left, the huts got knocked down.

When he was older, the company Grandad worked for used to work together with Tom Finney's company at Marks & Spencer stores all over Lancashire. One day, Grandad's boss told him to be ready outside Moor Park Avenue on Garstang Road to be picked up for a lift to Kendal.

'It's 7:15am, he's waiting patiently and sees this car coming down the road and thinks, I know that car, it's Tom Finney's.'

The car stops and Tom Finney asks, 'Are you going to Kendal?' Grandad says, 'Yes' and Finney says, 'well, I'm taking you.' And that was it.

Tom Finney drove my Grandad all the way to Kendal and apparently never spoke of football once, nothing at all! Imagine. That would be like Nugent giving me a lift to work today.

Aside from Sir Tom, Tommy Thompson and Willie Cunningham were Grandad's favourite players, and he was once in hospital in a bed next to Willie Cunningham. Willie was playing for North End at the time and they struck up a conversation which made Grandad's hospital visit much more pleasant.

For us, with Preston, it's more of a lifestyle thing going on North End. We've always gone religiously every Saturday. If we're not going to the away games, we're watching the telly together for the scores. For home matches we always leave at a certain time and, in the morning, Grandad gets us pies from Berry's on New Hall Lane so we have our pies and then head to Deepdale. That's our routine. Where we sit now, we have quite a lot of people who we talk to and that's really nice. It's a real community.

Photo (L to R): David Williams, Lucy Crompton.

LUKE 'TOMO' THOMPSON

BALL BOY

On Saturday 4th December 2019, North End played Luton Town at Deepdale. I was a ball boy and was positioned behind the goals at the Bill Shankly Kop. PNE were 2-1 up thanks to a Jayden Stockley goal, and with just a minute-or-so of injury time left, Luton were on the attack.

The ball went out for a goal kick to us so I picked it up. They'd been cheating the whole game and I don't know why their captain came over to me as it weren't even his ball. I refused to give it to him and instead walked away and handed it to our goalie, Declan Rudd, who took the ball and rubbed my head. At the end, their captain came over to me. I don't know what he said, he looked mad, but he shook my hand.

Well, the whole thing had been filmed and someone had posted it on Instagram. I have Instagram and I saw it on the PNE Official page so I put in the comments that I was that ball boy. Shortly after, my phone started going mad and I quickly got over 200 new followers. Everyone was ringing me and my family. People I don't normally speak to were pretending to be my best mate.

I was at my Nan's that night and she had her phone on full blast watching the footage. All I could hear was the commentary. I must've heard that commentary about 700 times because she kept on watching it and she was like, 'Oh, someone else has posted, and someone else, and someone else' It was class!

Then, as a treat, the main PNE Police Officer, PC Paul Elliott, drove me and two of my mates to the next home match in his police van. It was brilliant and they put the sirens on too.

I'm at high school now but I became a ball boy when my primary school teacher at St Andrew's recommended me and my friend to Michael Aspinall who runs the ball boys. My teacher knew I was a North End nut.

On a regular match day, we meet at the Sir Tom Finney statue between 2:30pm and 2:45pm then we all go into the ground.

As ball boys, we are given a full tracksuit, a hoodie, a waterproof coat and a massive coat. We sit in the Invincibles Stand before the game and watch the players warm up. The players always have two nets out for the warm up so when the nets come down, we go and get our stools and take our positions.

Michael tells us where we are sitting each game. I normally sit by the Invincibles, close to the tunnel, near where my family have season tickets so they can see me. At half-time, I run up and see my Grandad and he gives me something to eat. But I got lucky for the Luton match. It was the one game when they asked me to move. It was fate.

Before I was a ball boy, I used to go on with my Grandad, my Uncles and my Dad. The whole family supports PNE.

'I love everything about the club and my dream is to play for North End.'

I used to play centre-mid but I'm more of a winger now, a bit like Barkhuizen.

Supporting PNE and being a ball boy means everything to me. I don't know what I would do every other week without it. It's a big honour. I'm very lucky.

MARK WOODACRE

At home to Burnley on Tuesday 29th October, 1996 was my first game doing the drum. I was standing on the old Town End. I always loved the atmosphere on there.

It was pre-match and a man was wandering around near the drum area asking if there was anybody who fancied doing the drum. They wanted a second drum for that evening game and I just volunteered without thinking. The following Saturday at Deepdale, I actively went and found the drummer and asked if he wanted me to do this again, so it started from there and never really left me.

The club have been outstanding throughout the years and bought the first new drums of many decades last season. Back in the day, Craig Brown even gave me his mobile number and regularly came and spoke to me. They fully support the band with a purpose-built area and we have regular chats making sure we're on the same wavelength and all pulling the same way.

More recently, in this age of social media, there have been some interesting debates, but over the years many fans have enjoyed the drums and supported them wholeheartedly. For me, we had it perfect in the early noughties with me and another on base drums, Dave on trumpet – amazing trumpet player – and Crazy Dick on the snare drums; he was mad! An outstanding player who got the crowd going so easily.

I've taken the drum to a good few away games including the Millennium Stadium twice, a few trips to Wigan and Gillingham twice. In those two games at Gillingham we conceded 9 and scored 0. Painful days!

In 2001, for the first game of the season, I contacted Gillingham in advance and they said they were fine for me to bring the drum. We set off on the coach all excited, got to the ground only to be told, yes, the drum is welcome on the ground but no drumsticks allowed. They were considered offensive weapons.

I spent the whole game banging the drum with my hands and empty coke bottles. Not happy! And we go and get beat 5-0.

The hardest match I have ever been to and drummed on was in 2016 at home to Rovers. The anticipation was there all the week leading up to the game. Then sadly, the day before, we suddenly lost my Mum. My Dad was insistent we went on, saying we would only sit at home being upset otherwise and that Mum would have wanted us to be there.

I was drumming away and, as the first goal went in, I looked up sobbing but knowing I was with true friends and my best man. Ironically, we also played Rovers for the first home game after we lost my Dad in 2018. I can remember celebrating the goals and enjoying the win yet the sad site lower down the Town End of my Dad's empty seat was just horrible.

'For me, supporting PNE is life.'

I am Preston born and bred and they're my only team. Following PNE has been in my Dad's side of the family for years. As a child, I remember my Grandad being helped on by my Uncle. There's a running joke that he was ready to throw himself in the brook on Fulwood Hall Lane every time they lost which, in those days, was quite regular. I am proud that me and my children continue their tradition of supporting North End. I am also proud to say my Son now follows me in playing the drums on matches too.

Photo (L to R): Benjamin Van Parys, Mark Woodacre.

OLIVIA SIMPSON

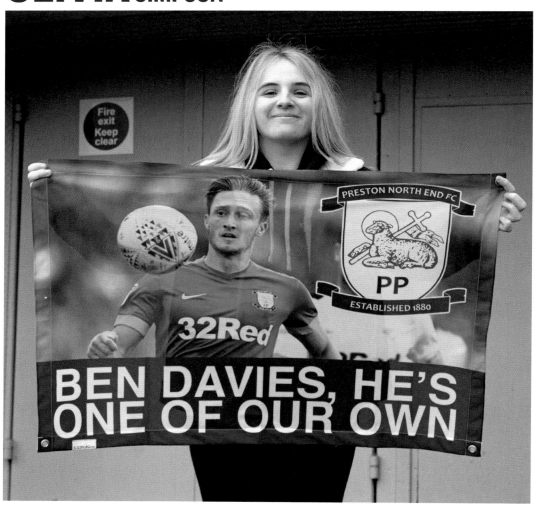

As a kid, I remember getting so excited when I spotted the famous PNE floodlights. My parents are Preston born and bred and following my local team just felt right.

Dad, who is a massive fan, brought me and my older Sister to Deepdale when we were young and from then on, I absolutely fell in love with PNE and football in general.

I used to play outside with my next-door neighbour. We'd play footy in the garden, tackling each other and practising penalties. He's a Liverpool fan but also had a PNE kit that I loved. I can't remember its exact year but it was a yellow and blue away kit and every time we played outside I nagged him to let me wear it.

My favourite PNE memory has to be watching Graham Alexander score that free kick against Charlton in his last game for the club. I was in the Sir Tom Finney stand with my Dad and best friend and remember Dad saying, 'Imagine if he scores this!' We all know what happened next. When it went in, I think in that moment I realised just how much a football club can mean to people, to the players as well as the fans.

For a few years, Ben Davies has been my favourite player and someone I've really looked up to. A while ago, I got a flag made with his picture on it and the words 'Ben Davies – he's one of our own.' I bring it to every away game I go to. The first one was Reading in 2019 which actually fell on my birthday and beforehand, unbeknownst to me, a friend of mine, a Reading fan, reached out to Ben on Instagram.

He told him I was going to be at the game with my flag for the first time and said, as it would be my birthday, it would be absolutely amazing if he'd able to give me his shirt from the match.

We lost the game, which wasn't a surprise given our record against Reading, and the players went straight down the tunnel, but later, when I got back on the coach

home, I received a message from Ben saying he saw the flag and had saved his shirt for me. So on the Monday I met Ben Davies at Deepdale and he gave me his shirt. Since then, he's spotted me quite a few times and even some of the other players know about my flag.

I work at McDonald's and one night Alan Browne came to the drive thru. I mentioned it and he said, 'Oh yes, I've seen that a few times. Ben absolutely loves it, trust me.' I feel really privileged to have such a relationship with my favourite footballer.

'For me, it highlights the type of club North End is, one where the gap between its players and fans is minimal.'

At the moment, I'm studying for a degree in Sports Journalism at UCLan. I've always had this passion for football and when I learned that Sports Journalism can be a career it was a no-brainer for me. My first published article was an assessment of Preston's first season in the Championship under Simon Grayson, and when I showed it to my parents they were so proud. Ever since then I've loved sports writing.

It sounds cliché but football and watching PNE is the only thing I really look forward to. In those ninety minutes, everything else in life is forgotten.

PAULA SUTTON-WHALLEY

Alex Dawson is my Dad's favourite ever player and we recently bought him a signed photo of The Black Prince. Dad used to go on North End when he was young and I just followed suit.

My earliest memory is of standing on the South Paddock and having pennies chucked at me over the metal fencing. I think this was around 1991 and, to be honest, I can't remember who we played but I do remember absolutely loving Gareth Ainsworth. I went on with some lads from school and there wasn't a big crowd that day, but I still got crushed against one of the barriers when North End scored. I got my first scarf that day too: a blue, white and yellow scarf which I've just lost!

The best game I ever saw was against Birmingham City in the play-offs. Seeing Trevor Francis spit his dummy out was one of the funniest things ever and winning was just the best feeling. I definitely cried tears of joy after that game. I went to the final with my Dad and was gutted we got beat but we had a brilliant day nevertheless. It was an amazing atmosphere in Cardiff and I am sure there were more North End fans than Bolton. I can remember seeing Frankie Worthington walking towards the Millennium Stadium and everyone chanting his name.

In 2005, my now-husband, Mark and I were on Sky Sports during the Play-Off Final against West Ham at the Millennium. We were near the front with Jacob, who was only around six months old and, although we were only filmed briefly at half-time, our phones went mad with friends and family messaging to say they'd just seen us on TV.

Mark and I got married on the 16th May 2008, and my family bought us a framed and signed PNE shirt. It was the best present ever. We also had a PNE themed wedding cake which my lovely friend, Dawn, made for us.

My Son, Jacob, has been going on since he was eight weeks old. His first game was at Deepdale on New Year's Day 2005 against Sunderland. Unfortunately, we got

beat 3-2. He's been on most home games since and has had a season ticket for most of his life.

Me and Jacob also try to get to as many away games as we can. We love the local derbies against Rovers, Wigan and so on, but my favourite away days are the London ones. We usually travel by train to London and always start off at The Moon Under Water on Leicester Square with breakfast and a pint; a pint for me, not Jacob. It's become a bit of a tradition now every time we travel down south. It can get a bit rowdy on the train there and back but everyone is always in good spirits, or maybe just full of spirits!

'I love North End and could never imagine supporting anyone else. They've made me laugh and cry and I've had some brilliant days following them, home and away.'

You've got to stick with them through thick and thin, and I just hope that I get to see them play in the Premier League, even if it's just for one season!

Photo (L to R): Jacob Whalley, Paula Sutton-Whalley.

PETE INGHAM

My Daughter lived in Santiago, Chile, a while back and I was fortunate enough to go and visit her with the rest of my family.

Along with Chile, we also took the opportunity to see as much of South America as we could, and on my list of dream places to visit was the famous Maracana Stadium in Rio, Brazil.

Before we travelled out to South America, I'd bought a copy of the graphic novel about the Invincibles of our beloved club – *Preston North End: The Rise of the Invincibles*. I bought it to read on the flight over and once I opened it, I couldn't put it down. I read it in one go!

Well, we made it to Brazil and I fulfilled a long-held ambition by going to the Maracana and watching the Rio derby played between Flamengo and Botafogo. It was an amazing atmosphere and during half-time, whilst queuing for a beer, I got chatting to a guy named Ernesto. We were talking about football and Ernesto, a passionate Flamengo fan, noted the North End shirt I was wearing and wanted to know more about the English game and PNE so I enlightened him with a little bit of our history.

'Then, in the spirit of world relations, I gave Ernesto the PNE scarf around my neck and, in return, he gave me his 'lucky' Flamengo cap.'

Ernesto was overwhelmed by the scarf and wanted to know more about our famous club. As it happened, I had my copy of *Rise of the Invincibles* in my rucksack and, after telling him about the great achievements of the Invincibles,

I decided to present him with the book. Suffice to say he was overjoyed!

It was such a fantastic experience to watch the Rio derby in the Maracana and made all the more special by meeting a true football fan and sharing tales of our beloved North End.

After the match, Ernesto vowed to wear my PNE scarf to all Flamengo games in the future and I promised to wear his Flamengo cap at matches too, so if you see anyone on Deepdale in a Flamengo cap, you'll know who it is!

So there you go, the Invincibles are now in Brazil. The book is a great way to teach people about the proud history of our fantastic club, but I often wonder how Ernesto coped with the Lanky twang.

Insert photo courtesy of Pete Ingham.

PETER HODGKINSON
'THE SPLASH' SCULPTOR

Yeah, my Dad used to take me on, on the West Stand with all the pipe-smoking old fellows with flat caps. We used to sit on the curved bit next to the Kop and look at all the hooligans.

I used to be more interested in what was going on over on the terraces with all the different characters. By the time I was a teenager, I was going on the terraces with me Cousin. There was a bit more atmosphere on there.

I went to sixth form college to study art, and my intention was to become a graphic designer but then I discovered there was such a room that you could make sculptures in and I started doing that. I applied to an art school in London at nineteen and that was it, I never looked back.

I was working in Halifax for a sculptor called Edward Cronshaw when it came up on Radio Yorkshire that Sheffield United were putting in a bid for the new Football Museum and their bid included statues of famous footballers. I knew North End were interested in the museum too so I contacted them and met with Bryan Gray at Baxi. He said, 'What do you want?' I said, 'I want to make this!' BANG, and I put a small bronze of Tom Finney on his table.

I'd made it based on the 'The Splash' photo which had won Photograph of the Year in 1956 and was such an iconic image. I think he was a bit taken aback. Still, he arranged a meeting with Ben Casey and it got put through the Football Museum as a project, but it then went back and forth on who was going to pay for it and took about eight years before I could begin.

When I started, I basically scaled up the smaller statue, made a frame, worked on it with clay and cast it. I've got photos of the whole process which should be a book in itself! I worked from photographs, and it was nine months in the studio then three months in the foundry.

At the end of July 2004, Sir Tom himself unveiled it which I thought was good. Finney had come up to my workshop to see it when it was halfway through and we had a laugh because he knew the area. He'd been there during the war when he was in the army. He said when he was on leave he went to a dance in one of the buildings near where I worked but I'm not going to mention where that was. It was a secret location.

'One of the things, when I actually got paid and got a cheque from North End, I didn't want to hand it to the bank. I wanted to put it on the wall. For me, it was the nearest to being in the team as I could be.'

I would say he was a very modest man. I don't think he was too pleased with the attention and I don't think he liked the idea of having a statue of himself. He always mentioned the other players, but he warmed to it. I saw him a couple of years after it had been unveiled. He was being filmed for TV and I was just walking past and wandered over and said, 'Hiya, Tom, do you remember me? I made that.' He just turned round and said, 'You know, it's very good. Who is it?'

RICK 'TLR' CARTWRIGHT

On the last game of the 1985-86 season we lost 4-0 away to Aldershot, finished second from bottom of the old 4th Division and had to apply for re-election. But to this day, that match remains one of my fondest PNE memories.

I was in the stand at Aldershot with my mate, Steve and we got talking to Jonathan Clark who'd been made caretaker manager after Brian Kidd's bad run of results. It was nearly full-time and Clark invited us to sit on the bench with him and Andy McAteer. Then when the match finished, he told Nigel Greenwood to give me his shirt, so it wasn't such a bad day for me, and I've still got the shirt!

My Dad first took me to North End for a match against Bradford City, that's my earliest memory. Then I took my Brothers on and, years later, my Grandsons and Nephew. I can remember the match when Alan Kelly injured his shoulder against Oxford and played as an outfield player with his arm in a sling. And I remember the days of Bobby Charlton being manager.

I actually have a sign from the old Preston North End Supporters Club up in my house. When AFC Fylde built their new ground at Warton, they bought some cabins off North End and in one of them was this old Supporters Club sign.

'I was painting the ground for Fylde at the time and was asked if I'd like the sign.

I didn't need to be asked twice!'

I go to all the away games. I think Coventry is my favourite ground as the setup is fantastic. I used to travel to away matches on the PSG coach, but then when I became disabled and passed my driving test I started driving myself to the games. I get many comments from fans about the North End badges on my wheels.

Preston North End are my one and only true love. I look forward to all the games – home and away, meeting old friends and making new ones. I have watched this club through the bad times, but it doesn't matter how bad they have been and how many times they let you down, I'll always be there. I'm North End through and through, and I've had some great moments with PNE, like the play-off finals, promotions and Wembley. Nobody can take those memories away.

Insert photo courtesy of Rick Cartwright.

STEPHANIE LAMBERT

You had two choices in our house: support North End or pack your bags! I'm one of three sisters and we're all keen supporters. Dad took us all to Deepdale as kids and my Mum has been to her fair share.

Mum is from Chelsea, and I think it would be fair to say Dad converted her to the cause too.

'Dad actually left his wedding reception to be with his first love: PNE.'

Mum obviously has the patience of a saint. It was 1987, home to Doncaster Rovers, and we lost 2-1. Mum likes to say, 'He won me, what more could he want?'

In those early days, The Garrison and Sumners were pre-game rituals. Dad would buy us bar snacks and play pool with us. The pub would be packed out. It was loud and rowdy and I fell in love with the atmosphere – the fans, the chanting, the laughter – it captured me.

Then it was the walk from the pub, down the steep hill along the sandy path. At the ground, balloons, horns, painted faces and streamers were commonplace. Everyone would stand and you could almost touch the away fans. Chants were back and forth the entire match. It was electric. Every game was like a mini carnival.

On Sunday 24th May 2015, we travelled to London on a coach, pulling over at the services and combining with other travelling fans for a huge rendition of Twist and Shout. I'm always on edge when North End play big games. I get nervous butterflies in my stomach, but for once, all those emotions didn't end up with my heart being ripped out of my chest. We completely dominated Swindon and you could sort of feel for their fans. We knew all too well what it felt like.

Don't get me wrong, we've seen good times, but like many fans during that era, we witnessed failed attempts, money troubles, countless managers and relegation so it was almost a relief to get that win at Wembley. Years of hurt and shattered dreams swept away with an emphatic 4-0 crushing of Swindon.

When that first goal went in, we lost it. Everyone did. You felt raw emotion in those stands – sheer jubilation. I remember feeling physically sick at some points. Everyone was nervous, but then the second went in moments later and belief set in. There was only ever one winner.

Garner turning to the fans and cheering as he shepherds the ball out of play will always remain iconic to me – a North End fan on the field, celebrating with the fans off the field. He knew what it meant, and I remember the crowd's reaction when he did that.

It was my Fiancé's first North End game. Not a football fan by any means but I just remember her shouting at the end of the day, 'I love football!' We'd took one of those blow-up sheep for a laugh and I ended up giving it to a lady sat in front of us. I later found out she still has it and its part of her memorabilia collection. It featured in so many pictures of the game. Sky Sports also used a picture of us all – proud Dad and all his girls at Wembley. That picture is now framed in each of our homes.

Supporting North End has given me irreplaceable memories with my family. It brings us together. Our club is different to most; Its traditions, our fans – we are like a huge, extended family, and being a part of that has helped me and my family create beautiful, everlasting memories that will stay with me forever.

STEPHANIE SLATER MBE

I can remember going to the Preston North End shop in the town centre every year to buy my Brother a North End shirt for his birthday. If I was lucky, I would get last season's shirt in the sale, if there was one to fit me. We loved wearing them with pride on holiday.

My first memory of meeting someone famous from PNE was when I was presented with a trophy at Preston Swimming Club by David Moyes who was then the PNE manager. I still have the photo from it and I can remember being so excited. I always dreamed of representing Great Britain at swimming and was determined to make this happen.

I went to St Cecilia's RC High School in Longridge and knew if you worked hard at your chosen sport it was possible to reach the top. Three ex-pupils had achieved this. Andrew Lonergan and Alan Kelly Junior both played for North End and Alan's brother, Gary, was also a professional goalkeeper. Alan and Gary's father, Alan Kelly Senior, was probably North End's greatest ever keeper, and my Mum told me about a match she watched in the 1970s when he went off injured. He then came back on and played outfield with his arm in a sling. I don't think he'd have been allowed to do that now.

We always had great banter within the GB team, especially if Preston were playing a rival team. Some team mates used to question why I supported North End. I always said how I would stay loyal to my home-town team, no matter what city I was living in and what division they may be in.

Unfortunately, I didn't get to visit Deepdale too often during my swimming career as I was not always living in Preston, and competitions were always held at the weekend so I didn't have a lot of free time. But whenever I got the chance, I would listen to the live commentary on Radio Lancashire.

On the 1st October 2016, North End played Aston Villa at Deepdale and I was the guest of honour along with my Mum, Dad and Brother. We won 2-0 and I can remember Chris Maxwell saving that penalty. Ex-PNE player, Tony Morley was there and he told us all about the days he was a teenager at Preston. It was really interesting listening to how much times have changed. After the match, I was then introduced to all the players, which ended an absolutely fantastic day for me and my family.

'I am very proud to say I come from Preston and support Preston North End. My Grandad used to tell me stories about watching the legendary Sir Tom Finney and my family have always supported the club, so it was natural for me to follow in their footsteps.'

I always look forward to following their highs and lows each week. It's a great hobby to have which is enjoyed by all my family.

Photo credit, Stephanie Slater, (L to R): Stephanie and Mum, Shirley..

STUART DAGGER

After we'd beat Chesterfield at Deepdale and got to Wembley with Beckford's phenomenal goal and Garner's penalty, when everybody was on the pitch, all of a sudden I turned around and Tom Clarke was stood in front of me.

Amidst all the cheering, all I could hear was, 'Get him up, get him up!' Now, I don't know what came over me, adrenaline or whatever, but suddenly I dropped to my knees into a squatting position, put my head between his legs, and lifted Tom Clarke up on my shoulders and started bouncing up and down singing, 'We are going up, say we are going up!'

'We all shared that one goal: to go up, the fans and players, and in that moment, when we were all together on the pitch, it was unbelievable.'

A huge moment. And now in the main entrance to the Finney Stand is that iconic picture of Tom Clarke on my shoulders. It's huge. What a memory. What a memory that was!

If you think, Colchester away, last match of the season, all we had to do was win, it was a given. But looking back, if we were offered the automatic place of going up or having that amazing day at Wembley, we'd all take Wembley.

I served in the RAF and after serving and being back home for quite some time, I was nominated to take the place of an old boy who carried the standard for Preston but was stepping down. So that's what I do now, and I have some civic duties which include carrying it at service funerals.

When Sir Tom sadly passed, with him being a part of Montgomery's Desert Rats during the Second World War, we were ordered to get the standards and stand outside the Guild Hall. When you're doing the standards you have to be very serious, regimental and po-faced but when Sir Tom came to a halt and paused in front of us and we were ordered to lower the standards, I couldn't help but have a tear in my eye.

Losing Sir Tom was a massive loss, not just to PNE fans but to Preston itself. I'm not old enough to have seen him play, but I can only imagine. If you think, Sir Tom and Stanley Matthews, two of the greats of the game, literally within twenty miles of each other, what great times that must've been! So to be just a small part of Sir Tom's final journey, not only as a PNE fan but as a Prestonian, was something very special to me and something I will always remember.

The day he left us, as soon as me and my young lad heard the news, we both automatically put our jackets and woolly hats on, bought some flowers and went straight to the Splash statue. It was pouring down and I remember my Son said, 'We should do something else, Dad.' Spontaneously I just walked into the Splash with my trainers on, took my woolly hat off and placed it on Sir Tom's head. Then later on, scarves, shirts and hats were all placed on the statue. It was very moving.

When I got married 25 years ago, we wanted to get married on North End but it was too expensive. So when we got married my Wife got my wedding ring made with PNE on it and whenever I take it off I always kiss the ring and say, 'Married to Wife and married to North End for life.' You see, PNE is in my blood. I always say if you cut me I bleed lamb's blood. I'm North End, end of.

TOM METCALFE

When North End returned to grass in 1994, I was the mascot for that first game back on turf. I got the job because the original mascot was ill and my Aunty, who was a secretary at the club, got me in as the replacement.

We beat Lincoln City 4-0. David Moyes was captain and I've vague memories of light blue paint and wallpaper in the changing room.

I also remember my Dad and Grandad kept trying to get a photo of me with Sir Tom but I was only four and kept running off after the ball. But I did meet Sir Tom later in life and got some photos. He was always such a gentleman. My Grandad always said when the defenders crashed into him, he would just roll his sleeves up and get on with it. My Grandad went on all his life and had lots of stories.

'I've become a father recently and I'm looking forward to taking my Son on and keeping the PNE flame going.'

When I was younger, I used to go on with my mates. It was a great escape from the stresses of life, especially the away games. I'd sometimes get wrecked and wake up thinking, *I spent over 200 quid there and I don't even remember the score!*

Once, we played Port Vale. It was the promotion season, a must-win game. We were two-up, then conceded two penalties in the last minutes to draw! I don't remember the end, I was absolutely trollied and sat on the steps instead of the seats. My mate has a photo from after the match; it's outside the ground and there's a massive fire bomb going off about twenty feet into the sky. I don't remember it – I wouldn't believe it but for the photo!

When I go on PNE now, I find some things surreal. As a musician, I've noticed this thing about accents. There's accents in music so there's a similarity, and I've noticed when fans are on PNE their accents get broader, all that 'cha' and so on. It's very interesting. Going on PNE is its own cultural institution, its own little world.

I remember when we were kids and someone saying, 'Yeah, my dad's letting me swear, but only for the Blackpool game!'

Football is very ritualistic. There's something else going on that's more than a bit of leather being kicked between two posts. The fact there's another town over there, trying to kick it through our goal and we're trying to stop 'em, it's tribal, something we've lost a bit in modern society. It helps our mental wellbeing, it's primal and something I'm very conscious of. Football fills that primal need, fills a void. It's us and them. Our tribe, their tribe.

There's nothing wrong with acknowledging that football is a safe representation where we can play out these primal feelings and, after the match, we all come together and shake hands, share a drink and understand we are all part of one world. It's very deep.

Following your local team, it's more like a religion – you don't get a choice. I know some people from Preston support Liverpool and so on and just watch Match of the Day, but they're not really fans. I'd call them hobbyists. It's not the same as going and supporting your local team. I learnt very early in life there are people who are just interested in football and then there are football fans, and I'm a football fan, and I follow PNE, do you know what I mean?

TOM WRIGHT

I started supporting PNE when I was four/five- years old, going on the games with my Mum who is a lifelong North End fan. It has passed down the generations of my family despite us all growing up and living on the wrong end of the M55.

Ever since the 2004-05 season, I've been completely hooked. I remember walking up the Town End and being so intrigued at the building of the new ground around us, and I began taking pictures at every match so I could compare them over time.

My favourite home game is the famous Blackpool match in August 2013. There's plenty to choose from but it's got to be the North West derby. It was such a special occasion for me given the importance of bragging rights (living there myself) and the sheer passion and rivalry between the fans.

'We hadn't played each other in a few seasons and they'd had the better few years compared to us, so to bring them back down to earth and let them know we're superior and the Pride of Lancashire made it so much better.'

Favourite away days? Blackpool in 2008 and Wembley in 2015. I'm also particularly fond of a couple of away games which, whilst not having much significance to the season, hold a lot of meaning on a personal note.

Middlesbrough away in 2019: This was unique for many reasons. At the turn of the year, I'd recently got back in touch with Ethan, an old friend of mine. We hadn't really been in contact for the best part of three years and he was back in England for a few days. As two lifelong North Enders, we decided to take the trip up to the Riverside.

It was a cold wet Tuesday evening and we wouldn't have had it any other way. PNE were pushing for the play-offs but, after a slow start, were on course to lose as Boro went into the break 1-0 up. Then Alex Neil changed things and brought on Manchester City loanee, Brandon Barker. Barker charged forwards, won a free kick on the edge of the box and Gallagher stepped up to score. We then went on to win with a Jayden Stockley header near the end.

Nottingham Forest away in 2018: North End were hit hard by injuries and results hadn't been too great, but the game finished 1-0 with a Louis Moult winner and an away end which erupted on that cold December day.

The day ticked all the boxes for me. I was with my soul mate, Naomi, and met some great North End fans who later really made me part of their group and made me feel welcome and at home with the North End faithful.

Another special moment was Louis Moult's winner. Louis himself had helped me on a personal level with people skills and gaining confidence and he supports charities close to my heart. I'd really formed a bond with Louis and his winner ticked off an amazing day.

Preston North End means the world to me and I don't make that statement lightly. It's a family club, and through it I've met the best people I could ever have hoped to meet! Their results make my weekend.

(Photo: L to R: Ethan Kirk Deleany and Tom Wright.)

TREVOR JOHNSON

I **was born in Lytham St Annes but grew up in Tardy Gate with my Mum and Brother, Karl. Mr May, an elderly neighbour, one day asked my Mum, 'Do you want me to take the boys to watch North End this afternoon, Maureen?'**

Her answer was, 'Yes.' That was half a century ago in 1971. I was nine and we beat Hull City 3-1.

I'll never forget walking up the steps on to the Spion Kop to see a green oasis in front of me. The autumnal sun was shining. I'd never seen grass like that; the pitch was immaculate. I was used to playing footy with my mates on the Red Rec in Tardy with tank tops as goalposts.

'David Nugent's bowler hat, remember that? Well it wasn't David Nugent's bowler, it was mine, and still is.'

But it's the one he wore after scoring away at Watford. I lobbed it onto the pitch when he was celebrating and he duly picked it up and popped it on. Incidentally, I bumped into Nuge in Sharm El-Sheikh many years later in a bar. We got chatting and I said, 'Do you remember wearing the bowler hat at QPR?' And he quite rightly put me right and said, 'Nah, mate, it was Watford away.'

Back in the day, we travelled to all the away games in my Mini EBV53W. After Cambridge away, when we guaranteed promotion, all the cars, minibuses and other forms of transport were driving round with scarves and flags hanging outta the windows whilst blowing their horns. I'd none of that, so off came me jeans and I let them fly! How I got away with some of the stuff I'll never know.

My favourite one was the Lancaster M6 Junction sign. I'd had my eyes on that road sign for a number of years. I used to pass it every other week whilst playing golf at Bentham and was waiting for us to play them lot. Then when we came outta the hat in the League Cup I thought, *this is my chance to sort that bloody sign out*. We played them on the Monday. Tommy scored. Sign sorted on the Wednesday on my way to golf. RESULT.

North End Soul? Back in about 1978/79, I was sat in art class at Todd Lane School. In front of me, Elaine Carter had a bag slung over her chair with Wigan Casino patches on and stuff. The teacher said, 'Today it's all about logos. I want you to draw a logo using pencil, crayon or paint.' Most opted for Coca Cola, Swan Vesta or Embassy No.1's etc. but I copied the Northern Soul: A It's A Way of Life logo off Elaine's bag but altered the wording to 'North End Soul'. Many, many moons later my mate, John Billy, mentioned something about having some t-shirts made with the 'North End Soul' logo on so I said, 'Leave it with me.', and the rest is history.

The logo has been seen on the terraces now for nearly twenty years and also all around the world. I've posted clobber to places such as Australia, New Zealand, Canada, USA, Germany, France, Belgium, Norway, Finland, Isle of Man, South Korea –or maybe North Korea – Thailand and the Philippines, to name but a few. Oh, and Chorley.

The brand isn't quite as big as Nike and Adidas but it may be one day. I've managed to get it on TV a few times and I sponsored Lee Cartwright one season too. I can't remember him getting any gear off me but I did end up with a shirt of his though. North End Soul: it's a way of life.

VIPUL PATEL

I've lived in Preston since I was five years old. The first house we lived in was on Bullfinch Street in Deepdale which meant on Saturdays, when Preston were at home, we could hear the crowd cheering the team on.

Growing up, we were a cricketing family and never went to watch PNE but I always used to wonder what being on the terraces was like.

The first match I actually went on was with my eldest Son, Raj, when he was four. It was against Oldham Athletic and I remember the buzz around the ground before the match and how excited Raj was at being able to go inside the ground. It was a 1-0 win so a great start for our North End experience.

'Although we are fairly new supporters, we already have favourite memories. For my Son, Aaryan, it is the 3-2 win against Blackburn.'

Being 2-0 down then coming back to win showed how well the team supported each other and then there was all the fans celebrating wildly in the stands. Also my three boys and my Dad came to the match so it was extra special at the final whistle.

One of my own favourite memories is of the Burton Albion match back in 2018. Beforehand, there was much anticipation and I remember the crowd being in good voice in the sunshine. Preston could still make the play-offs and Burton could be relegated. That day, we went through all the emotions: early goal scoring opportunities missed, Robinson scoring, then Burton scoring, and finally an injury time winner! Although PNE didn't reach the play-offs, in the end it was good to finish with high hopes of reaching them next time around.

Then there is the Rotherham away match on New Year's Day 2019, even though it was a loss. The trip was great fun as my Dad, Raj, Aaryan and I drove to the stadium. During the journey we saw several cars with PNE scarves and, as the boys in the back waved their scarves to the other cars, we could see the cheering going on. At the game, we sat quite close to the pitch and at full-time Paul Gallagher came over to the stand and gave his shirt to a young fan. It was a lovely touch from him.

Players like Gallagher and Daniel Johnson are a credit to the club as when we have seen them, they've always had time to spend with the kids. And then after the match, to top it off, Aaryan and Raj ended up on Twitter due to the PNE photographer, Dave Kendall, posting a photo of them. They were elated!

This season, Aaryan and I travelled to Nottingham Forest for the 1-1 draw. We stood up all through the match for this one and Aaryan had to stand on the seat which he thought was 'amazing!' We chatted to fellow supporters who were all really friendly and inclusive and shared their different experiences of grounds around the country. For me this is what PNE is all about.

I believe PNE is a family-orientated club which is inclusive of everybody. I am proud to say I support them. The club and its players are so involved with charity and community work and give a lot back to Preston.

Photo (L to R): Aaryan, Bhim (top), Vipul, Raj.

WENDY SKERRITT

PNE are and always will be my team. Once it is in your blood it's there for life, through good times (been a few) and bad times (too many to remember).

The thrill I get when I'm with the fans is the same now as it was at my first match in 1977. That day, I went on the Kop as a fresh faced fourteen-year-old with my boyfriend at the time and his mate, and we are all still good friends today.

My first away match was against Notts County. Nobby Stiles was manager and we had Roy Tunks in goal. We went by coach, it was Mercer's or Craven's, and I travelled to that match with another school friend, Diane Peel (now Speakman). Her dad, Ken Peel was a massive PNE fan and his enthusiasm for PNE rubbed off on me. Ken sadly passed away last month in his 90s and I managed to get his name on The Gentry flag that was displayed in the stands for the first game without fans because of COVID-19.

In November 1980, we played West Brom away in the League Cup. They were a 1st Division side managed by Ron Atkinson and we were in the 2nd Division. We had drawn the first game 0-0 then drawn the replay 1-1 at Deepdale, and so a week later played a second replay at the Hawthorns.

West Brom had some class players in their squad back then, players like Tony Godden, Brendon Batson, Remi Moses, Gary Owen, Bryan Robson, Peter Barnes and Cyrille Regis. It was a close game but we lost 2-1 after extra time. I remember being crammed in the away end with thousands of PNE fans. It was a night match and I can just remember the noise of the PNE fans who sang their hearts out for the entire game. It's probably on a par with the atmosphere at Deepdale when we beat Birmingham City in the play-off semi-final in 2001.

That's one of my favourite memories – beating Birmingham in the 2nd leg after being 1-0 down from the 1st. It took

me a week to get my voice back! And then there's beating Torquay United 4-1 in the 3rd Division play-off semi-final 2nd leg in 1994 after being 2-0 down from the 1st leg.

'It was our last game on the plastic and I can see now the pitch being ripped up after the match and lots of our supporters taking pieces home with them.'

In 2000, I was on the Flag Market after we'd won the Division 2 title under David Moyes. I was celebrating our promotion with thousands of other PNE fans when I received a message from one of my friends who was working in the Harris asking if me and my friends would like to come up to where the players and VIP guests were gathered on the top steps. So we explained to the police who were manning the barriers keeping the fans back that we'd been invited up.

The police then lifted us all over the barriers and threw us in the back of a Black Maria (everyone thought we'd been arrested) and drove us to the side door where we gained entry. It was just fantastic and I got my photo taken with Moysie and the Cup.

When the pictures of the North End team with the trophy were published in the Lancashire Evening Post you could see me with my camera stood by the pillar on the left hand side. That moment will live with me until my dying day. It was one of the best days of my life.

PRESTON FANS
ARE THE BEST,
THEY'RE THE
GENTRY.

-ALAN BALL SNR, 1970

WE'RE THE ONE & ONLY NORTH END

Preston 1
Blackpool 0
M6   SUPER
TOMMY CLARKE
87mins

WAITING FOR GLORY

RED ROSE BOWL

24-lane tenpin bowling alley in the heart of Lancashire

50 Greenbank Street, Preston, PR1 7PH

Enjoy a **fun-filled** day of tenpin bowling with prices starting at **just £4**, and enjoy **food and drink** and our **amazing arcade!**

Book **NOW** to avoid disappointment!

1 Game: £4
2 Games: £7
3 Games: £9

Family hour (max 6):
£22.50 - 1 hour
£32.50 - 2 hours

OPENING TIMES

Weekdays:
10:00-23:30
Friday and Saturday:
10:00-00:30

Follow our **Facebook** for **exclusive offers** and to **book online.**

Fully licensed bar and diner

f **Red Rose Bowl**

📞 01772 429947

🌐 www.redrosebowl.com

✉ redrosebowl@outlook.com

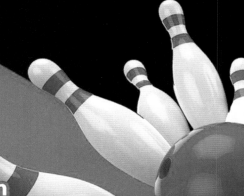

No job too big.

Client: Preston North End

No job too small.

Client: Royal Mail

the chase creative consultants
thechase.co.uk

ACKNOWLEDGEMENTS

Firstly, a thank you to Katie Simpson for all your hard work on this project. Also thank you to Sam Combes for your work. In turn, this book would not have been possible without the early support of Debbie Jane Williams. Thank you, Debbie. Sincere thanks go to Graham of The Princess Alice, Ben Casey of The Chase Creative, JD Sports and Phil Butterworth of Red Rose Bowl for their adverts. Another thank you goes to Ben for writing a fantastic foreword. I'm grateful to Jeremy and Rossella and all the printing staff at L.E.G.O. in Italy.

I'm grateful to Ben Rhodes and PNE for supporting this book and allowing me to photograph parts of the stadium, and to Paul Bradley for your patience and time. Sincere thanks to Tom Drake, Matthew Brown and the PNE Community Team, and especially to PNE photographer, Ian Robinson. Thanks to Rob Cross for colouring our fantastic cover photo, and to Peter Holme and Weibke Cullen of the NFM archives for the image. Also to Gillian Parkinson and Dave Seddon of the Lancashire Post. For various reasons, my gratitude goes to Steve Hargreaves, UCLan Publishing, John, Paul and Tom of Withnells Brewery, Dennis Higgins, Andrew Wilson, Bob Clare, Eyosefy of Kwick Stitch, John Billington, John Roper, Mark Naylor, Eddie Mayor, Gary Mounsey, Dave Nelson, John Kelly, Dave Seddon, Leanne Naylor, Jonny Richardson, James Arnold and the Harris Museum, John Wilson, Bev Taylor, Jo Harwood, Blacky, Paul Whelan, Carolyn Mercer, Adrian Murrell, John Gillmore, Mark Inglis, Stephanie Lambert and Peter Paddock, Janice Falconer, Lindsay North, John Jackson, Martin Atherton, Trevor Johnson, Tom Smith, Alan Kelly, Mark Naylor, Simen and the Norwegian Branch, Sergio, Shiho and Keith McIntosh.

I'm appreciative to all the shops and booksellers, and everyone who has supported and helped promote Invincible Books in the past – every gesture helps and is always appreciated.

To my wonderful colleagues in the MRI Department at RPH, thank you for your friendship and encouragement. Thanks to my friends, with special mentions for Bernard, John, Tize and Tomás. To my Godparents, Pam and Jack, and finally for their unwavering help and support my family: Dad, Bridget, Sharon and Gary, Bernadette and Winston, Michael, James and Jayden, and last, but always first, Mum.

PHOTO CREDITS

Cover photo used with the permission of the NFM and coloured by Rob Cross. Twitter: @RobCross247.

Front & back endpapers, credits and thanks: Turnstile image, Daniel Gray. 1938 FA Cup Final ball, property of Tom Smith. PNE ring, property of Stuart Dagger. PNE flag, whisky bottle, early PNE badge and West Stand sign, property of Gary Mounsey. PNE rattle, property of John Jackson. Old pavilion mural image, Gary Harris-Newsham. Contents page, programmes image, Eddie Mayor.

Gentry Page, credits and thanks: Pie Muncher and RTC fanzines, property of Dennis Higgins. 'One & Only' flag, property of J. Fish. M6 sign image, Trevor Johnson. Fulham ferry image, Shaun Lewis Walker, 'Waiting for Glory' flag image, Blacky (PNE Mooching page).

Great Relations chapter title photo, images and thanks: Bill Shankly photo, Steve Cowell. Tom Smith photo, Tom Smith. Sir Tom Finney and Alan Kelly Snr photos, Gary Mounsey

This book is dedicated to all fans and players who have been injured or lost their lives in conflict.

First published in 2020 by Invincible Books Limited

www.invinciblebooks.co.uk

ISBN: 978-0-9956023-1-1

Published by Invincible Books Limited in 2020

Design, interviews and original photos by Michael Barrett

Design, editing, typesetting by Katie Simpson
For enquiries, contact katiesimpsonedits@gmail.com

Printed by L.E.G.O., Italy. www.legogroup.com

PRESTON NORTH END FC

PP

ESTABLISHED 1880

PNE
FOREVER

WEST STAND